BECOMING
TRUSTWORTHY
WHITE ALLIES

BECOMING TRUSTWORTHY WHITE ALLIES

Melanie S. Morrison

Duke University Press *Durham and London* 2025

© 2025 MELANIE S. MORRISON. All rights reserved
Project Editor: Lisa Lawley
Typeset in Portrait and Proxima Nova by Copperline Book Services

Library of Congress Cataloging-in-Publication Data
Names: Morrison, Melanie, [date] author.
Title: Becoming trustworthy White allies / Melanie S. Morrison.
Description: Durham : Duke University Press, 2025. | Includes bibliographical references and index.
Identifiers: LCCN 2024057231 (print) LCCN 2024057232 (ebook)
ISBN 9781478032434 (paperback)
ISBN 9781478029090 (hardcover)
ISBN 9781478061281 (ebook)
Subjects: LCSH: White people—United States—Attitudes. | Anti-racism—United States. | Racial justice—United States. | Race awareness—United States. | Civil rights workers—United States—Anecdotes. | United States—Race relations. | LCGFT: Anecdotes.
Classification: LCC E184.A1 M677 2025 (print) | LCC E184.A1 (ebook)
LC record available at https://lccn.loc.gov/2024057231
LC ebook record available at https://lccn.loc.gov/2024057232

Cover art: Backgrounds courtesy Adobe Stock/arwiyada and valiantsin.

For April Allison,
with gratitude for your wisdom,
and your anchoring love.

Contents

Foreword JENNIFER HARVEY		ix
Introduction		1

I. INNER WORK

1	Becoming Trustworthy White Allies	13
2	Memories of the 1963 March on Washington	19
3	Qualities and Commitments of White Allies	25
4	A Misguided Struggle	27
5	Why an Antiracism Seminar for White People	31
6	This Is What Accountable Relationships Look Like DIONARDO PIZAÑA AND MELANIE S. MORRISON	41
7	Dear White People	47

II. ANCESTRAL INVESTIGATIONS

8	Cultural Envy	51
9	Genealogy as Spiritual Practice: Reflections on My White Ancestral Work	57

10	Why We Must Remember: A King Descendant's Reckoning with Her Enslaving Ancestors	61
11	A Just Reckoning: Forging Deeper, Truer King House Narratives	75
12	Letter to My Great-Great-Great-Grandmother, Elizabeth King Shortridge	87

III. LEGACIES OF LYNCHING

13	Soul Splitting	95
14	Researching Injustice: Telling the Story of Legal Lynching in Jim Crow Birmingham	101
15	Trayvon Martin, the Legacy of Lynching, and the Role of White Women	113
16	At the Hands of Persons Unknown: The Verdict in the Michael Brelo Case	123
17	"The Fierce Urgency of Now"	127

IV. STAYING POWER

| 18 | What Will It Take for White People to Stay the Course? | 133 |
| 19 | In the Time That I Have Left | 149 |

Acknowledgments	153
Notes	155
Bibliography	163
Index	171

Foreword

JENNIFER HARVEY

Jennifer Harvey is author of Antiracism as Daily Practice: Refuse Shame, Change White Communities, and Help Create a Just World *and* Raising White Kids: Bringing Up Children in a Racially Unjust America.

Whenever I have the chance to talk about Melanie Morrison, I usually begin by saying, "Melanie was my mentor—years before she even knew who I was." The truth is that countless others—and I mean *countless*—could give a similar testimony.

I have heard people say, "I didn't know 'doing our own work' was something white people could do—and then I saw her antiracism seminar with that exact name." "I'd never seen someone speak so boldly and publicly about white responsibility, while moving so deeply and accountably in interracial relationships—and I wanted to become able to do the same." "You know what? I participated in one of the cohorts Melanie designed and facilitated through Allies for Change and my life was never the same. Thank god."

And now this book.

Becoming Trustworthy White Allies is not just another book about white people and racism—though we do need more good books and meaningful work in that realm. This book is an offering. It is an offering by one of the elders of white antiracist activism who has finally made time to put her experiences, knowledge, and wisdom to the page and has pulled together several of her essays, lectures, and stories into one place for all of us to read.

For decades Melanie has made visible the path for white antiracism. She has done it as a teacher and activist-practitioner. Following the wisdom and guidance of her own antiracism elders, Melanie became acutely aware that white people have deep inner work to do as they seek to engage more consistently and effectively in the collaborative work of racial justice.

This book is a gift because it engages and explores concepts and questions that are important in white antiracism spaces. For example, Melanie gives us insight into the ways she has wrestled, as a white person, with questions of ethnicity and genealogy and then takes us through a powerful narrative of how those questions have led her to the work of repair and reparations. She also stresses how crucial it is for white people to develop and nurture relationships of support and accountability with Black, Indigenous, and other people of color as we work for racial justice.

This book is a gift because those of us who are white and longing for a more racially just world and seeking to play a meaningful role in bringing that world into fruition need to hear, learn, and remember the stories of our elders. We need to learn from the wisdom of elders who have been engaged in this long-haul journey; people whose legacies made a way for us to locate ourselves and find one another in the journey.

Melanie is precisely one of those humans. She is one of the most authentic and powerful sages when it comes to whiteness and racial justice, and this book gives us the chance to learn from and with her.

And yet, like everything else Melanie Morrison creates, *Becoming Trustworthy White Allies* is not self-referential. This book is far more than a collection of reflections on Melanie's own life and the various stages of growth and creativity she's journeyed through as she walks this path.

Melanie is a white lesbian feminist. She describes her own positionality with critical self-reflection and then roots it deeply in broader and larger landscapes such as ancestral investigations, theories of racial development, legacies of lynching, contemporary legal crises, and more. She makes it possible for her readers to see how each of our own unique, distinct, and particular stories are also part of this larger landscape—and, by so doing, compels us to ask, "What is thus necessary in this journey, now, *for me*?"

Let me just give you one example that gripped me. As Melanie writes about coming to terms with the legacies of her enslaving ancestors, she teaches us about the ways that slavery has personal effects in our collective lives. She challenges us to understand that the work of creating a different kind of now and tomorrow requires that we first grasp how our lives are embedded in the legacies of white supremacist violence.

I'm gripped because I, for one, am serious about being part of creating a different kind of now and a radically different tomorrow. And I know many of us share that longing.

The final section in this book is titled "Staying Power." Whatever unfolds among us in the coming years in this land, we will need staying power. *Becoming Trustworthy White Allies* provides nourishment and connection for that lifelong journey. It makes visible and transparent the kind of extended work we must undertake in order to move beyond guilt and shame and work toward becoming trustworthy white allies.

Introduction

Thirty women filled the meeting room the first night of the Women's Theological Center (WTC) Anti-Racism Training Program. As we introduced ourselves one by one around the circle, I was grateful, awestruck, and intimidated to be entering this new learning community. The WTC had brought together a racially diverse group of women with years of engagement as activists, educators, and leaders of local and national movements for racial justice.

With three colleagues, I had flown from Michigan to Boston to attend this intensive four-day workshop in June 1994. I was a forty-five-year-old United Church of Christ minister who had served three churches before cofounding Leaven, a nonprofit organization, with my mentor and mother, Eleanor Morrison. Launched in 1987, Leaven provided education, resources, and training in the areas of feminism, spiritual development, and sexual justice. In the 1970s, my mother designed the first sexuality courses taught at Michigan State University and wrote three books about teaching human sexuality to undergraduates, before being ordained in the United Church of Christ at age fifty-five. She was a skilled and brilliant designer of experiential group process, and I wanted to work as her apprentice, learning those skills firsthand.

In Lansing, Michigan, we created a space for grassroots feminist reflection, study, and dialogue that explored the wisdom and vitality of spiritualities rooted in a passion for justice. We also traveled the country speaking to and consulting with nonprofit, educational, and religious organizations as a mother-daughter team, one of us an out lesbian and the other a fierce heterosexual ally.

It was good and needed work in a time when women and LGBTQ people faced unrelenting violence and discrimination, but our work had gaping holes because the resources and training we provided as two white women often failed to center the lives of Black, Indigenous, and other women of color. Having been confronted by women of color about those dangerous and harmful omissions, we enrolled in antiracism trainings they recommended, including the one that brought us to Boston in the summer of 1994.

On the second day of the WTC antiracism workshop, the lead facilitators, Donna Bivens and Nancy Richardson, introduced a guest speaker who had worked for years as a coach and consultant with historically white organizations that sought to become racially equitable. She presented a graphic tool that displayed the characteristics of organizations on a continuum from monocultural segregated institutions to antiracist multicultural institutions, and she described the challenges organizations faced as they worked to uproot patterns of unearned privilege and grow equity.

When the guest speaker paused to welcome questions, I raised my hand and asked if she could please share examples of organizations that had attained the goal of becoming a "transformed organization."

She shook her head and said, "No, I can't do that."

"Oh, you don't have to provide the name of the organization," I explained. "I understand that would be a violation of professional ethics. I'd just love to hear some stories about organizations that have reached that stage of development."

Shaking her head from side to side more emphatically, she replied, "No, I'm sorry I cannot provide those stories because I have never witnessed them. I can tell you about meetings I have experienced when all the voices at the table were heard and honored, and people dared to invite conflicting perspectives and do the hard work of acknowledging harmful behaviors. But too many organizations stop short of the long-haul process required to institute substantive and sustainable change."

I imagine I was frowning and squinting with bewilderment as she responded, thinking to myself, *She's got no examples to show us? That is so disheartening.*

Unable to accept what the speaker was revealing, I raised my hand again and exclaimed, "But, if there aren't examples or models, how can we have hope about this work?"

Sitting near me, Donna Bivens turned to face me head on and paused before speaking. Later I wondered if she had been questioning whether I was worth the patience and energy required to make herself heard. I was immensely grateful she decided to take the risk.

"This is the work, Melanie," she said, leaning toward me. "You will encounter resistance and roadblocks. This work is not easy. It's a constant struggle. That has been the experience of people of color for centuries in this country. We work for justice, experience victories, and are inevitably met with white backlash and resistance. But we have forged communities of love and care that nurture the spiritual strength to keep hope alive, and we carry on. That is the work, Melanie."

I thanked Donna. Later that evening, I scrupulously recorded in my journal every word Donna had spoken, not wanting sleep to steal even a portion of what she had given me. Thirty years later, her words still live in me, having taken deeper root through my own experience of facilitating with other skilled and tenacious colleagues of color.

I now understand that investment and commitment are required from everyone in organizations if they are to undergo significant change. Leaders who embrace equity work eventually leave, retire, or die. Boards of directors change personnel and alter their vision. New generations of employees are hired and need additional training. Most disturbing of all is to witness what can happen when the equity work is forsaken: how it took years of concerted effort to move the organization forward, but sometimes only months for organizations to backslide and devolve.

As I have reflected on the way Donna spoke to me that night, there is another part of her message that has taken root in me. I believe she wanted me to reckon with the deep work I and other white people need to do if we are going to develop the stubborn tenacity, relentless commitment, and spiritual strength to carry on.

It was the WTC workshop and subsequent conversations with colleagues of color that led my mother and me to launch an antiracism seminar for white people in the fall of 1994. We chose the name Doing Our Own Work because we had heard these colleagues say there is work that you, as white people, must do with and for each other. They encouraged us to start an intensive antiracism program that would help move white people through the places we so often get stuck, including obliviousness, denial, fear, guilt, and shame.

Doing Our Own Work was designed as a supplement to, not a substitute for, contexts in which people of different races strategize together about the ways racism must be confronted and dismantled. The seminar was envisioned as a way station that would help build the capacity and knowledge that white people needed to work in solidarity with people of color.

The first Doing Our Own Work seminars were held in Eleanor Morrison's living room, an inviting space large enough for the circle of ten participants and two facilitators who gathered weekly for eight evening sessions. As word spread about this new seminar, a larger meeting space was needed to accommodate the growing number of registrants and the ever-changing curriculum. We rented meeting and lodging space at a nearby retreat center so that participants from other towns and cities could attend, and the Doing Our Own Work curriculum continued to deepen and expand to six full days of seminar held over a three-month period.

Utilizing documentaries, assigned readings, small and large group discussion, structured exercises, and guest presentations by colleagues of color, Doing Our Own Work was a highly interactive experience. A number of the topics addressed in this book are inspired by the questions we wrestled with during this six-day seminar:

- What daily practices do I need to develop that will help me acknowledge and confront the unearned privileges I am granted as a white person?
- What can I do to interrupt and dismantle the habits, practices, and policies that protect those unearned privileges?
- What are creative and constructive approaches to interrupting racist comments and behaviors in my encounters with white coworkers, neighbors, friends, and family members?
- What can I do to develop and nurture authentic and mutually enhancing relationships with people of color?
- What does it mean to be in accountable relationships with people of color when working to interrupt and dismantle systemic racism?
- When is it okay, and when is it inappropriate, for me to express my grief and tears about racism?
- What would pride in, or love of, my culture look like, and feel like, as a white person who strives to be antiracist?
- What would it mean to love my white self, my white body, in ways that do not reek of superiority?
- What have I received from my ancestors (related to race or racism) that needs healing?

- What can I do to assist in that healing?
- From what or from whom do I draw inspiration, strength, and courage in my antiracism work?

My experience in this seminar repeatedly confirmed that when white people find a learning community like Doing Our Own Work, they experience a profound sense of relief, recognizing that they are not alone. We often heard Doing Our Own Work participants declare, "I didn't know how or where to voice these questions. I feared being misunderstood or judged. It gives me heart and hope to find others with whom I can commiserate, struggle, vent, be challenged, and find support."

In March 2000, Leaven celebrated the opening of its own retreat and study center, and Doing Our Own Work was one of the programs we offered. Located on forty acres of land near Lyons, Michigan, the Leaven Center was forty-five minutes from both Lansing and Grand Rapids, two hours west of Detroit, and four hours east of Chicago. The meadows, woods, riverbanks, and facilities at the center offered a beautiful, hospitable, and restorative environment. We intentionally chose not to call it the Leaven Retreat Center because the word *retreat* implied escape from the world. The Leaven Center was designed for people engaged in the fray—for social justice activists, artists, and educators who needed a place that offered rest, nourishment, and revitalization for their bodies and spirits. For those committed to working for social change, the struggle is long, the danger of burnout great, and the temptation to despair frequent.

The Leaven Center offered a wide array of workshops, retreats, and seminars facilitated by outstanding leaders from different communities in the United States and Canada. We were committed to making the center physically and financially accessible to all who wanted to come. We purposely kept registration costs low, provided ample scholarships, and rented space for a modest fee to social justice organizations. The Leaven Center gained a national reputation as a place that brought social justice activists together for difficult but crucial conversations, popular education, community building, cross-fertilization, and the strengthening of alliances and coalitions.

In every aspect of the organization, from staffing and board membership to the selection of workshop topics and presenters, we sought to make the center a welcoming space for people of different races, ages, abilities, gender identities, sexual orientations, and spiritual traditions. It wasn't a perfect start. We made mistakes that were cringeworthy and called for correction. More than once, we had to pause the planning for a specific program until all voices and perspectives were justly represented.

As director of the Leaven Center, I experienced firsthand the challenges organizations face as they seek to uproot patterns of unearned privilege and grow equity. My innate desire to accomplish tasks efficiently and speedily was frequently upended by a staff person, board member, or volunteer who summoned us to slow down and invite more people into the conversation and decision-making when we were on the brink of violating a cardinal rule of equitable practice: Nothing about us without us. For example, until disabled people were involved in the design and implementation of accessible practices, Leaven could not announce that its events were compliant with the Americans with Disabilities Act. The expressed intention to do the right thing is never enough. People who have the lived experience of marginalization and exclusion are the ones who will determine what is just accommodation and inclusion.

I loved the work of helping to found, develop, and administer the Leaven Center. I learned invaluable lessons about the long-haul work of implementing and sustaining equitable practices and programs. And yet I also loved to collaborate with colleagues envisioning, designing, and facilitating antioppression workshops and seminars. After giving ample notice of my intention to step down, a new Leaven Center director was hired in December 2007, and I launched Allies for Change, a national network of social justice educators who led workshops and trainings for organizations seeking to deepen their commitment to social change.

The Allies for Change network was diverse not only racially, but also in terms of gender, age, disability/ability, sexual orientation, and class background. We designed programs and workshops that addressed the intersections of racism, sexism, ableism, heterosexism, and other systems of privilege and oppression. We referred to ourselves as Ally Training Partners because all of us were committed to the lifelong work of understanding where we stand in relation to systems of privilege and oppression, and to building authentic and accountable relationships across difference.

Depending on the focus and audience of the training, we worked together in different constellations of team members. Most of our workshops were led by a racially diverse facilitation team for groups of racially diverse participants. As Ally Training Partners, we held these core beliefs and principles in common:

- Genuine and lasting change involves both personal and institutional transformation. One without the other is an insufficient and truncated form of change.
- Understanding where we stand in relation to systems of privilege and oppression, and unlearning the habits and practices that protect those systems, is lifelong work for all of us, without exception.

- We can become as passionate about dismantling the systems from which we benefit as we are about eradicating the systems that oppress us.
- Allies are not solo acts; their social change work is always rooted in collaboration, humility, and accountability.
- The interior journey into silence, meditation, inner wisdom, and deep joy is inextricably linked to the outer work of social change.
- Truth telling, confrontation, and anger can be paired with compassion, humility, and forgiveness.

Action and reflection formed the heart of every Allies for Change program with the goal of equipping participants to become knowledgeable and compassionate agents of structural change. We invited participants to engage in rigorous social and historical analysis, and to practice strategies for interrupting oppression. Recognizing that we need spiritual resources to sustain this work, Allies for Change programs utilized a creative array of teaching models and media. Through storytelling, poetry, music, and deep listening, we sought to cultivate a loving and truth-telling community that allowed us to explore the complexities of our own experience and open our hearts to others.

As I approached my seventieth birthday in 2019, I decided to step back from the work of facilitating social justice workshops and seminars in order to make ancestral research and writing a full-time priority. The yearning to investigate my ethnic and cultural origins was awakened by the ancestral questions we explored in Doing Our Own Work and further intensified when my Aunt Harriet (my father's only sibling) shared a startling revelation in 2008, two years after my father's death and just months before I launched Allies for Change. I was visiting Aunt Harriet in Raleigh, North Carolina, when she informed me that I am a direct descendant of enslaving ancestors who lived in Montevallo, Alabama, a small town thirty-five miles south of Birmingham. She also mentioned that the former home of those ancestors, now known as King House, is centrally located on the University of Montevallo campus. According to local legends, it is a haunted house.

Since that day, I have been haunted by Aunt Harriet's revelation. Just shy of my seventieth birthday, I decided to acknowledge my sense of being pursued by Montevallo by embarking on a journey into ever deeper involvement with people in Montevallo, both living and dead, constantly asking myself: *Why do I feel compelled to take this journey? What does this reckoning with my ancestral past require of me?*

I have made numerous trips to Montevallo to search for archival records, meet with local historians, and deepen relationships with Montevallo residents committed to unearthing suppressed stories about the Indigenous removal and enslavement that occurred in that region.

At the University of Montevallo, that work is being undertaken by the Peace and Justice Studies program in partnership with the Montevallo Legacy Project—a community action group devoted to giving voice and visibility to people of African descent in Montevallo. It has been a privilege to work collaboratively with the Montevallo Legacy Project and the students and faculty in the Peace and Justice Studies courses as we seek to forge deeper, truer narratives about King House history and the legacies of slavery. I have been invited to deliver lectures on campus and to mentor students who are seeking to break the relative silence surrounding King House history. They have created written, audio, digital, and video resources that tell a different King House story.

This process has reaffirmed my belief that, despite well-funded efforts to restrict the teaching of slavery and systemic racism, there is a deep yearning in this nation for truth telling. I have heard that yearning expressed repeatedly by University of Montevallo students. In online and class discussions, students are engaging in self-reflection and dialogue about the pain, distress, and anger they feel as they examine more deeply the exploitation, dehumanization, and brutality of slavery. They are vulnerably giving voice to their shock and embarrassment to have walked past King House innumerable times oblivious to the violence that was meted out within those walls. They are grappling with the social, economic, and political legacies of slavery that continue to create systemic inequities and disparities.

This book is a collection of articles, speeches, essays, and stories written during the past twelve years while serving as executive director of Allies for Change, helping to mentor a new generation of Doing Our Own Work facilitators, and working with antiracist colleagues in Montevallo. Some of the pieces reflect on encounters, workshops, and events that occurred decades ago, including my experience attending the 1963 March on Washington as a fourteen-year-old.

In pulling the pieces of this book together, I had two primary groups of readers in mind. I am writing for white people who are deeply troubled by the corrosive persistence of systemic racism and who long to develop the capacity and resiliency to be agents of change where they live, work, study, and volunteer. I am also writing for white people who seek to move through places where they often get stuck so that they can step up with humility, courage, and consistency to participate in movements led by people of color and help move other white people to greater antiracist awareness and action.

The title of this book—*Becoming Trustworthy White Allies*—needs to be placed in its intended context lest it should sound like I am offering white people a step-by-step blueprint or template. As I state in chapter 3, "Qualities and Commitments of White Allies," I believe the word *ally* should be regarded as a verb rather than a noun because it represents the commitment to show up, take action, and be in right relationship. Being an ally is not a static reality, once and for all achieved. Neither *trustworthy* nor *ally* are words that white people can claim for themselves. Black, Indigenous, and other people of color determine who their allies are and when trust has been earned.

I also believe that learning what it means to be trustworthy white allies is a lifelong journey, rife with risks, regrets, growth, and joy. In the essays, stories, and speeches included in this book, I reflect on the work we can and must undertake if we seek to become trustworthy. For example, I discuss working through shame and guilt, nurturing truth-telling relationships, challenging practices and policies that protect white privilege, moving out of social segregation, doing the work from a place of self-love, and staying on the journey.

Many of the pieces in this book are story based, and some are autobiographical, in the hope that my experiences will intersect and resonate with your own. I share with you the mistakes I have made, the wisdom that colleagues and mentors have shared with me, the repair I have sought to enact, and the strength and hope I have found working with others to nurture antiracist communities of love, support, and accountability. Through it all, I have found solace and encouragement from the words Donna Bivens so generously spoke thirty years ago:

> This is the work, Melanie. You will encounter resistance and roadblocks. This work is not easy. It's a constant struggle. That has been the experience of people of color for centuries in this country. We work for justice, experience victories, and are inevitably met with white backlash and resistance. But we have forged communities of love and care that nurture the spiritual strength to keep hope alive, and we carry on.

I. INNER WORK

1

Becoming Trustworthy
White Allies

In the early 1990s, an African American friend and colleague, Lynnette Stallworth, challenged me to critically examine why I, as a white woman, so often looked to her as an expert on racism, depending on her to call me out or advise me when racist words, behaviors, or policies were at play.

"What happens when I am not here, Melanie?" Lynnette asked. "How are you, as a white person, holding other white people accountable? How are other white people doing that for you? Racism is a white problem, and it is long past time for you all to do your own work!"

I was stunned and convicted by her challenge. I had to acknowledge that I and many of my well-intentioned white friends did not have vocabulary to talk about racism in an everyday kind of way. We were frequently mired in feelings of guilt. When we encountered racism, we could not be counted on to speak up and confront it. Too often, we fell mute, became confused, reacted with defensiveness, or simply wanted to disappear. I could see that I was not trustworthy, especially when things got hot.

To understand what it means to be white in America and break the silences that surround it requires arduous, persistent, and soul-stretching work. Sadly, too many of us stop short of that deep work. We assume that our good intentions and eagerness to help are enough. We come into multiracial gatherings or organizations expecting to be liked and trusted. But trust isn't something we are granted simply because we finally showed up. Trust must be earned, again and again. Or better said, we need to become trustworthy white allies, people passionately committed to eliminating systems of oppression that unjustly benefit us.

Lynnette's challenge inspired me to launch Doing Our Own Work, an antiracism program for white people who seek to deepen their commitment to confronting racism and white privilege where they live, work, study, and worship. Doing Our Own Work is designed as a supplement to, not a substitute for, contexts where people of different races discuss and strategize together how racism can be confronted and dismantled.

It has been an honor and a joy to do this intensive work for the past two decades with hundreds of people from communities across the United States and Canada. Out of that work, I want to share some reflections about the deep and sustained work I believe white people can and must do if we want to be effective and trustworthy allies in the struggle for racial justice.

Own That We Are "Raced"

As white people, we have inherited an intergenerational legacy of silence, looking away, pretending not to notice, and numbness to pain. As Robert Terry said, "To be white in America is not to have to think about it."[1]

As a beginning exercise in Doing Our Own Work, we ask participants to take out a blank piece of paper and write this incomplete sentence at the top: "To me, being white means..."[2] They are given three minutes to list as many things as they can think of to complete the sentence. We then invite them to take out a fresh sheet of paper and write the same incomplete sentence at the top: "To me being white means..." Again, they have three minutes to list their responses. By the third and fourth time they are asked to complete this same sentence, some people are laughing nervously, others are scowling, yet others put their pens down and stare out the window.

"This was really hard," is the most common feedback. "If the sentence had been, 'To me, being a woman means...' I could have written pages. But I had nothing to say about this."

"At first I wrote really negative things, and then I made a list of privileges I have as a white person. The third time, I tried to go deeper, write about things I had never thought about or allowed myself to feel before."

In the conversation that follows, we talk about why we so seldom must think about our white racial identity when people of color have to think about and navigate race and racism day in and day out. We also reflect on what might happen if we paused several times a day and asked: "What does it mean that I am white in this situation, in this encounter? What am I failing to see? What is the work I need to do, here and now, as a white person?"

The challenge Lynnette issued in the early 1990s I've heard restated many times since by other people of color in my life who've said, "I appreciate that you want to understand my experience as a person of color in this country. But what I most need from you, Melanie, is that you begin to understand your own. I need for you to do the strenuous work of understanding what it means to be white in America. Unless you do that, you are dangerous."

In my experience, those of us who are white are far more apt to identify people of color by their race than we are to identify ourselves as white. Too many of us have not begun to explore how we feel about being white or how racism has shaped our lives. This means we frequently enter multiracial conversations and collaborations expecting people of color to open up and share how racism affects them without being willing to share an equivalent level of vulnerability and self-disclosure.

Make Privilege Visible

One meaning of being white is that we are granted unearned privileges and structural power simply by reason of our race, without regard for our personal attitudes, values, and commitments. Peggy McIntosh has noted that "privilege is a fugitive subject" about which white people were meant to remain oblivious.[3] Making privilege visible to ourselves and others requires constant vigilance. Without that vigilance, we are indeed dangerous because we behave like dinosaurs that drag a large tail behind us. Unable to see the tail, and convinced of our good intentions, we are oblivious to the havoc we wreak as we move through the world, knocking people over and flattening things in our path.[4]

How do we do this? By presuming we can speak for others, imposing our mission and outreach projects on others, discounting as "ungrounded" the fears and criticisms voiced by people of color, dismissing their pain as overreacting, accusing them of "playing the race card" when they call us on our oppressive behavior, and then shifting the focus to our hurt feelings.

Making privilege visible is only the first step. In our spheres of influence, we need to interrupt racism by challenging the practices and policies that protect privilege and keep it in place. We can use privilege to ensure that power is more equitably shared. We can shine a light on every program, ministry, and endeavor we are engaged in, asking: Whose voices are being sought out and heard? Who decides what is right, beautiful, true, and valued? Whose cultural perspectives are overrepresented and whose are underrepresented? Who is seen as important to the mission and who is seen as less important?[5]

Work Collaboratively with People of Color

As we seek to make privilege visible and interrupt racism, it is essential that we do this in partnership with people of color. Otherwise, we may do more harm than good. If we charge ahead, eager to impose our solutions and interventions, we replicate old patterns of missionary zeal as we plant our ally flag and run the risk of jeopardizing those we are presuming to "help."[6]

Our work as allies must always and everywhere be grounded in humility, collaboration, and accountability. This means becoming engaged in organizations led by people of color, respecting the priorities they identify as strategies for change, and sustaining our engagement over time. It also means learning about the ways people of color have resisted racism long before we arrived on the scene. By showing up consistently and acting collaboratively, we have the possibility of developing authentic relationships of mutuality and accountability with people of color.

Nurture Truth-Telling Relationships

Becoming trustworthy white allies is something we cannot do by ourselves. We need the support and challenge of relationships where there is a shared commitment to speak our truths and hear each other all the way through, no matter how uncomfortable the revelations may make us. This, too, takes time and effort. Such relationships need to be sought out, nurtured, and sustained.

Work Through Shame and Guilt

When denial gives way, and the breadth and depth of racism are acknowledged, a profound sense of shame or guilt can consume white people for a time. While shame and guilt are not the same, both can surface in us as we awaken to the devastating realities of racism. Neither is particularly useful to people of color because both have the effect of turning the spotlight on white people once again. For example, white people may seek forgiveness from people of color to lessen their shame. This request can be toxic for people of color if the focus is the feelings of white people rather than the continuing inequities of racism.

I do not believe it is possible for white people to circumvent shame and guilt, but we can learn to move through those feelings and into something deeper and more productive. The critical question is what we do with those feelings and the discoveries that birthed them. As Audre Lorde said, "If [guilt] leads to change then it can be useful, since it is then no longer guilt but the beginning of knowledge."[7]

Do the Work from a Place of Self-Love

When Lynnette and other people of color challenge me to understand what it means to be white, I don't think they are asking me to be consumed by guilt, shame, or self-hatred. On the contrary, I believe they want to be met by white people who love themselves and others enough to do the deep work of truth telling and healing so that together we might repair the breaches that racism creates. I am utterly convinced that those of us who are white will not be able to keep showing up, resist checking out, or stay in difficult yet essential conversations across racial difference if we cannot come from a place of self-love.[8]

We need to love ourselves and others enough to forge new ways of being white in this world by nurturing an antiracist identity. We need to recover the stories of white ancestors who resisted racism and worked with people of color to keep hope alive by creating change. Their witness and resolve can strengthen our own.

We need to feel, claim, and give voice to our grief, distress, and rage at racism. The hunger and thirst for racial justice must be our own. Otherwise, we will be driven by the desperate need to seek approval and love from people of color. Writing about her work as a Latina multicultural educator, Lillian Roybal Rose says, "I tell white people in my workshops that I expect them, as allies with power in the oppression of racism, to act justly and not dominate, regardless of the fact that we may never love them."[9]

Stay on the Journey

I believe it is possible to become trustworthy white allies if we are willing to move out of our comfort zones, risk having our assumptions challenged, our lives disrupted, and our way of viewing the world transformed. Most important is the commitment to stay on the journey. Unlearning and interrupting the habits, practices, and policies that keep racism and white privilege intact is lifelong, life-giving work, never done once and for all.

2

Memories of the 1963 March on Washington

I pretended not to notice my mother at the water's edge calling me to come ashore. During supper I had begged her to take us to the beach before sundown. Ducking under the waves, I headed one last time for the sandbar. When I came up for air, I changed my mind and headed for shore. Everett McNair was talking with my mother, gesturing emphatically about something I knew I didn't want to miss.

Whenever Everett McNair appeared on the beach, I found some excuse to be nearby. He told captivating stories about things that mattered. Everett and his wife, Irene, had a cottage up the hill from ours, and they came every summer from Alabama, where he worked as chaplain of Talladega College. My father had told me that Talladega was the oldest historically Black college and that Everett, as a white man, considered it a great privilege to serve as chaplain.

Everett was a tall man in his mid-sixties. He seemed immeasurably old to me, as a fourteen-year-old, but his seniority only enhanced the prophetic powers I attributed to him. He had witnessed tumultuous upheaval in the South as the fortress of segregation was crumbling, and he had been one of the subversive agents working for that change.

As I grabbed a towel and threw it over my wet shoulders, I heard my mother complaining that my father had left for home in East Lansing to write his sermon and attend a trustee's meeting at the church he pastored.

"I don't know why Truman can't take one or two Sundays off in the summer," Mother said.

"I can relate to that behavior," Everett said, shaking his head and laughing. "I've been a workaholic much of my life. One of the advantages of coming all the way from Alabama each summer is that I have no choice but to turn things over to others while we're gone."

Turning to me, Everett asked, "When do you go back to school?"

"I start high school next Tuesday," I replied, hoping my voice didn't betray my considerable anxiety about going to a new building full of students older than me.

"Do you think the three of us would have time to take a trip before you start school?" Everett dug his foot in the sand and kicked it in my direction.

I looked at my mother, wondering if they'd been talking about a trip. She hunched her shoulders.

"Tomorrow morning," Everett said, "tens of thousands of people will be converging on Washington, DC, for the largest civil rights march in this nation's history. What are we doing here on this beach in Michigan? We should be on our way to Washington."

"How in the world would we do that, Everett?" Mother asked.

"I've talked with Irene, and she's more than happy to have Wendy and Stephanie stay with her at our cabin. It's only eight o'clock right now. If we head out by ten, we can make it to DC by the time the march starts."

Mother turned to me. "What do you say, Melanie—should we do it?"

"Yes!" I shouted, thrilled to be included.

"Okay then," she declared. "Give me a couple hours, Everett, so I can pack and get things around for us and the girls."

It was close to midnight before we got on the road. Everett wouldn't accept my mother's offer to take our car. He insisted there'd be more room in his Impala to stretch out on the back seat to sleep. When Everett was driving, Mother frequently asked if he was having difficulty seeing the road or staying awake. It was unusual for her to relinquish the wheel, and I knew she was anxious about how fast we were going. Everett seemed oblivious to it all, and the Impala sailed over the Pennsylvania mountains through the night toward Washington, DC. I rode shotgun most of the way, far more interested in hearing Everett's stories than wasting time sleeping.

"My dad told me that you were arrested last year at a sit-in. What was that like?"

"Well, we didn't experience the kind of violence they suffered at the Woolworth's counter in Greensboro, North Carolina. We didn't have hot coffee poured on our heads or lit cigarette butts burned into our arms."

"That's what happened in Greensboro?" I asked, horrified, trying to imagine how I'd ever summon the courage to continue sitting at a lunch counter while being burned and scalded.

"Those students in Greensboro got badly beaten up. They sure did." Everett reached for his mug of coffee and apologized for having nothing to offer me. I assured him all I needed was his story.

"Well, we'd certainly been spat upon often enough in demonstrations, so we feared the worst. The police were waiting for us when we arrived at the drugstore. They moved in.... We went limp.... They had to drag us to the paddy wagons. My head hit the pavement a few times as they dragged me, but none of us was seriously injured. We decided to refuse bail and stay in jail."

"Weren't you afraid?" I asked.

"Oh yes. But we had each other to lean on. We prayed and sang together. We filled that jail with songs! Singing and praying kept our spirits high and pulled us through."

Everett started humming. Then, right there in the car next to me, he sang out,

> Ain't gonna let segregation turn me round,
> turn me round, turn me round.
> Ain't gonna let segregation turn me round,
> I'm gonna keep on walkin', keep on talkin',
> marching up to freedom's land.

"Did you return to the lunch counters when you got out of jail?" Mother asked, sliding to the edge of the backseat so she could be part of the conversation.

"City officials imposed an injunction barring any form of demonstration in the city. We were pretty demoralized at first, but lo and behold, within a couple months, the public library opened its doors for the first time to Negroes and the merchants agreed to integrate their lunch counters."

"That is so cool!" I shouted. "You won!"

Everett laughed and patted my arm. "Well, in a way we won, Melanie. But there is so much work yet to be done."

"I know," I said, gravely, regretting that I wasn't old enough to be involved in sit-ins.

Staring at the taillights of the car ahead of us, I imagined my body going limp and my head hitting cement as I was dragged toward a paddy wagon with sirens blaring and lights flashing.

We were thirty miles from Washington, DC, when the traffic began to slow to a crawl. Fortunately, we'd stopped for a predawn breakfast, wanting to give ourselves plenty of time to make it to the Washington Monument Mall by the 10:00 a.m. starting time. By 8:30 a.m., traffic was excruciatingly sluggish. At 10:00, we were at a complete standstill at least half a mile from the Mall.

"What are we going to do now?" I moaned. Panic flooded me. Had we come all this way to be stuck in a traffic jam?

"The only thing we can do," said Everett, grinning at me and pointing out the window. "We're going to leave the car right here by the curb and walk...no, run with all those people headed to the Washington Monument."

"Just leave the car?" My mother asked with alarm.

"Yes." Everett opened his door and motioned for us to follow. "I see no other option."

My mother grabbed my hand, and we took off running with Everett leading the way. When we joined the throngs near the Monument, a volunteer handed us signs ("We Are Marching for Jobs and Freedom") and motioned for us to veer to the left. Everett took my other hand, and we fell into line, moving with the swelling crowds of people clapping, chanting, and singing. Volunteers in bright-colored T-shirts directed us to a wide passageway between two rows of towering trees running parallel to the reflecting pool.

When we finally came to a stop, we were on the other side of the trees in the bright August sun, not far from the edge of the road directly in front of the Lincoln Memorial. Turning around, I saw thousands of people standing shoulder to shoulder for what seemed like miles, stretching all the way back to the Washington Monument and lining both sides of the massive reflecting pool.

Huge platforms for the speakers, singers, and camera crews had been constructed halfway up the steps of the Lincoln Memorial. Just as Everett had experienced during his time in jail, music wrapped around us and filled the air that afternoon. I sang full-throated and swayed to songs led by Harry Belafonte, Bob Dylan, Joan Baez, and Peter, Paul, and Mary. My parents often played albums by Odetta, so I clapped and threw my arms in the air when she stepped to the microphone and her deep voice rang out: "If they ask you who you are, tell them you're a child of God." When Mahalia Jackson sang, I closed my eyes and let the music wash over me as the exquisite harmonies of people around me rose and fell. "I've been 'buked and I've been scorned, I've been talked 'bout sure as you're born."

Many of the speakers were unknown to me, but I recognized the name Norman Thomas when he was introduced. My father often spoke of his respect and admiration for Norman Thomas, who left the ministry to engage in full-time activism as a socialist and pacifist crusader for racial justice. I was thrilled to see Jackie Robinson in person and hear him declare, "We cannot be turned back."

I knew we were standing in a choice location, but as the day wore on, I felt envy for people who were sitting at the edge of the reflecting pool, splashing water on their faces, arms, and legs. We hadn't thought to bring lawn chairs, so we had to stand or sit on a small patch of grass.

By midday, the high August sun was scorching and the humidity thick. People were milling and fanning themselves while speaker after speaker came to the microphone. Volunteers came through the crowd periodically asking us to move back so that ambulances could reach people fainting from the heat.

Suddenly, people rose to their feet and pointed at the stage. "It's him. It's him!" The milling and talking ceased. A hush fell over that great assembly. No one moved. I could swear that even the babies stopped crying as Dr. King began to speak.

"Five score years ago, a great American, in whose symbolic shadow we stand today, signed the Emancipation Proclamation...."

Children were hoisted onto their parents' shoulders. People leaned into each other, clasping hands, locking arms.

"This momentous decree came as a great beacon light of hope to millions of Negro slaves who had been seared in the flames of withering injustice...."

Dr. King's lilting cadence rose and fell across the reflecting pool and ricocheted off distant buildings. Black elders on every side of me raised their palms toward the heavens as they responded to his words:

"Yes. Yes."

"*It came as a joyous daybreak to end the long night of their captivity....*"

"That's right, now."

"*But one hundred years later, the Negro still is not free.*"

"Speak the truth, speak the truth."

Dr. King declared that the Constitution was a "promissory note" guaranteeing all citizens the unalienable rights of life, liberty, and the pursuit of happiness.

"*It is obvious today that America has defaulted on this promissory note insofar as her citizens of color are concerned.*"

The crowd roared, "Yes, it has. Yes, it has."

Dr. King pledged to carry the struggle forward until justice reigned and the dream was fulfilled. The crowd responded rhythmically, echoing words and phrases, calling out to him to take his time and preach the dream.

I listened intently to his words, but I wasn't watching the speaker's stand. I was captivated, enthralled by the people in front, in back, and on all sides of me. Young and old, weeping and laughing, embracing each other, raising their arms and fists high, their faces turned to the sky.

"When we let [freedom] ring from every village and every hamlet, from every state and every city, we will be able to speed up that day when all of God's children, black men and white men, Jews and Gentiles, Protestants and Catholics, will be able to join hands and sing in the words of the old Negro spiritual, 'Free at last! Free at last! Thank God Almighty, we are free at last!'"

At the conclusion of Dr. King's speech, Bayard Rustin and A. Philip Randolph challenged us all to take a pledge, promising we would carry the message of this revolution back to our communities. I felt ready and eager. People reached out to join hands. I stood between my mother and a young Black man with a son perched on his shoulders. I held their hands tight as A. Philip Randolph read the pledge slowly, emphasizing each and every word of this solemn vow.

"I pledge to carry the message of the March to my friends and neighbors back home and arouse them to an equal commitment and equal effort.... I will work to make sure that my voice and those of my brothers ring clear and determined from every corner of our land. I pledge my heart and my mind and my body unequivocally and without regard to personal sacrifice, to the achievement of social peace through social justice."

"How do you pledge?" asked Bayard Rustin.

With that mighty throng of 250,000, I threw my head back and shouted, "I do pledge."

3

Qualities and Commitments of White Allies

Those who strive to be allies are people passionately committed to eliminating the systems of oppression that unjustly benefit them. The word *ally* should be regarded as a verb rather than a noun because it has to do with action, showing up, and right relationship. It is not a static reality, once and for all achieved. Nor is it a label that people with privilege can claim for themselves. People who are targets of oppression determine who their allies are.

Arduous, persistent, and soul-stretching work is required of white people if they want to understand the privilege they carry, nurture authentic relationships across race, and act collaboratively with Black, Indigenous, and other people of color (BIPOC) to dismantle racism. Good intentions and eagerness to help are not enough. Consistency and long-term commitment are essential. Trust must be earned, again and again.

If you are a white person who strives to be an ally, your consistency and commitment will be reflected in a willingness to do the following:

- Educate yourself about racism.
- Work at understanding that racism is far more than personal prejudice.

- Listen to, believe, and learn from BIPOC when they describe their experience of racism. Stay present and do not rush to offer solutions.
- Amplify the voices of BIPOC.
- Examine and challenge your prejudices, stereotypes, and assumptions.
- Educate yourself about the unearned privileges, advantages, entitlements, and access to structural power you have been granted because you are white.
- Work with others to interrupt the habits, practices, and policies that protect white privilege.
- Act collaboratively with BIPOC to dismantle racism.
- Be open to challenge and correction by BIPOC and white allies.
- Be concerned about the impact of your words and actions, as well as the intentions that lie behind them.
- Work through feelings of guilt, shame, and defensiveness to understand what is beneath those feelings and what needs to be healed.
- Learn and practice the skills of challenging oppressive remarks, behaviors, policies, and institutional structures.
- Cultivate a spirit of personal and cultural humility.
- Nurture authentic and truth-telling relationships of accountability with BIPOC and white allies.
- Get involved in organizations and movements led by BIPOC, respect the priorities they identify as strategies for change, and sustain your engagement over time.
- Hear the anger, rage, and grief that BIPOC express about racism without judging or policing their feelings.
- Feel your own anger, rage, and grief at racism.
- Bring your full self to the work of racial justice.
- Stay on the journey for a lifetime.

4

A Misguided Struggle

"Uncharacteristically subdued" is how Lynnette described my body language the day I told her that April and I had decided to purchase the property in Lyons, Michigan. Lynnette knew that we had been dreaming for years of launching a retreat and study center. And that land would be a perfect setting. The owners had developed a wildlife habitat with meditative pathways that wound through woods and fields of goldenrod, and ran alongside the Grand River.

April and I had been in the throes of intense discernment for weeks, and Lynnette was delighted to hear that we were preparing a written offer.

"Congratulations, Melanie! This is huge. How come you're not dancing around the house? Last month, showing me photographs of that land, you cooed like a woman in love. What's going on?"

"I don't know, Lynnette. Maybe the reality of it all is sinking in." I stirred my coffee and reached for cream to stall for time. "After all, it's going to take a tremendous amount of work to launch this place from scratch."

"Hard work has never stopped you before." Lynnette smiled and winked at me. "You've been dreaming about this for years."

"I know, I know." I scanned the room, searching for the words. "I think that maybe, as April and I grow clearer about doing this, I am increasingly aware that we can do it because of the privilege we possess."

Lynnette's eyes narrowed. "Say more."

"Well, you know, not everyone has that kind of..." My voice trailed off as I took another sip of coffee.

"That kind of what?" Lynnette motioned for me to keep talking.

I could feel my cheeks growing hot. I was stammering, hoping to convey my message without having to really spell it out. Lynnette rarely finished my sentences for me or accorded me shortcuts. She expected candor, an attribute I'd often admired and praised. But now I wanted to shout, "Oh come on. Help me out here. You know what I am trying to say."

Lynnette leaned back in her chair, crossed her arms, and waited.

"I'm just trying to say that, well, I'm aware that my white skin privilege probably plays a crucial role in acquiring this property."

"Uh huh." Lynnette nodded and waited.

"I mean...you know, it might not be safe for Black women to start that kind of center on a gravel road in rural Michigan."

"Yes," Lynnette said with a dispassionate matter-of-factness. "It doesn't often happen that Black women come into possession of land through inheritance or other means, including land contracts. And, yes, it might not be safe for me to start a center like yours in a rural area. So, what does that mean to you?"

What does that mean to me? Didn't I just say what that means to me? I was trying to read Lynnette's face—certain she was concealing anger at the inequity she just named.

"Well, I'm struggling with that awareness. With that unfair advantage."

Lynnette shook her head and looked away. When she spoke again, she stared at me, her head cocked slightly to the left.

"I get the sense that you think you don't deserve this opportunity. Is that true?"

I nodded. Then stood up and paced the room, searching for the right words.

"I'm sick of white people who keep telling me this was 'meant to be.'" I raised my hands, mimicking a gesture toward the heavens. "They say it with such pious certainty, calling it karma or God's will or the universe offering itself to us...."

"Uh huh," Lynnette said, nodding. "Doesn't it sometimes feel like that to you?"

"Yes, but they never acknowledge that white privilege might also be playing a role," I said, hoping Lynnette would grant me at least a nod of recognition.

Instead, she hunched her shoulders and asked, "Why do you need them to say that?"

I sat down again and stared at the floor. *Why is this so hard?* I asked myself. *Why can't I make myself understood?*

"I have a problem with those declarations about blessings," I replied. "The same problem I have when people talk about how blessed they are to have good health, food on the table, or to be living in a free country. As though it's all a divine gift. As if privilege plays no part in having access to those things."

Lynnette leaned toward me, speaking with quiet deliberation: "Could it be that this opportunity is both a blessing and a privilege? Does it have to be either/or?"

I was speechless. With patience, Lynnette posed more questions.

"Melanie, do you think that it would serve me, a Black woman, if you turned down this incredible opportunity, this blessing? Do you think I'd benefit from you and April not buying the land or developing the center because white privilege is at play?"

I closed my eyes, hoping to hear her questions more deeply. Lynnette continued purposefully, compassionately, like a teacher who takes pity on an earnest but uncomprehending student.

"I think your struggle is misguided, Melanie. Nothing you do is devoid of white privilege. You take that with you wherever you go. In whatever you do. The question is not whether it's right or wrong for you and April, as white women, to buy that land and start a center. The question is: What kind of center are you are going to create? Will it be a place of refuge, renewal, support, and community for all women? Will it foster and support the well-being of women of color as much as it fosters and supports the well-being of white women?"

This conversation took place on a Saturday morning in late September 1995. Two weeks later, April and I signed the land contract and began preparing in earnest for the move. I will always look back with wonder and gratitude at Lynnette's piercing questions, sharper than any two-edged sword, able to judge the thoughts and intentions of my heart. Those two hours at her kitchen table freed me from useless hypervigilance and strengthened my resolve to work with colleagues of color every step of the way as we envisioned and birthed the Leaven Center.

5

Why an Antiracism Seminar for White People

For twenty-six years, I had the privilege of codesigning and cofacilitating Doing Our Own Work (DOOW), an intensive antiracism seminar for white people who seek to deepen their capacity to claim and embody an antiracist identity, understand the privilege they carry, and interrupt racism where they live, work, study, and volunteer. My mentor and mother, Eleanor Morrison, and I founded DOOW in 1994 while serving as codirectors of Leaven, a nonprofit organization based in Michigan dedicated to nurturing the relationship between spirituality and social justice.

The decision to launch DOOW arose from conversations with colleagues of color who challenged us to develop a rigorous antiracism seminar that could interrupt the repetitious and hurtful behaviors white people often exhibit in multiracial spaces: denial, defensiveness, tearful shame, and a white savior mentality. It was their experience that white people's growth in consciousness too often occurs at the expense of people of color. It was long past time, these colleagues insisted, that white people begin to "do their own work."

Doing Our Own Work was designed as a supplement to, not a substitute for, contexts in which people of different races strategize together how racism must be confronted and dismantled. Nothing can take the place of face-to-face contact, dialogue, and collaboration between people of different races. But too often, those of us who are white come into those racially diverse spaces carrying unexamined privilege and emotional baggage that gets projected onto people of color in ways that disrupt, sidetrack, and undermine the collaborative work that needs to be accomplished.

In designing an intensive learning community for white people, my mother and I sought advice, counsel, wisdom, and warnings from colleagues of color who recognized both the need for DOOW and the dangers inherent in all-white spaces. We continued to enroll in diversity, equity, and inclusion workshops and institutes led by multiracial teams to stay abreast of new methods, information, and resources. We assumed that we would always be colearners with DOOW participants. We intended to design and facilitate the DOOW sessions not as antiracism experts but rather as fellow seekers on a lifelong journey.

During the first two years of designing and leading DOOW, while experimenting with different formats and time frames for the seminar, we became convinced that DOOW needed to be six full days in length. We wanted people to live this seminar, not just take it. Deep and transformative work cannot be done in a daylong training or even a weekend training. Those of us who are white have inherited not only unearned privilege and conferred dominance, but also an intergenerational racist legacy of obliviousness that manifests in silence, looking away, pretending not to notice, and numbness to feelings of pain and anger.

We limited enrollment to twenty participants to ensure in-depth reflection, dialogue, and community building. We also decided the seminar should be three months in length. That way participants could gather once a month for two days; return to their respective communities, taking note of how racism was at play in their daily lives and contexts; reconvene for the next two days of DOOW; share what they experienced and learned in those intervening weeks; and be ready for an even deeper dive with the DOOW learning community.

We could not be certain that people would be willing to devote that much time to a seminar that promised to be a deep dive. We feared the length and intensity might frighten and intimidate prospective participants. To our surprise and delight, people responded to the invitation saying they longed for an intensive and sustained learning space where they could acquire the analysis, in-depth reflection, conceptual tools, and behavioral skills necessary to become more effective allies with Black, Indigenous, and other people of color.

The first two days of DOOW were devoted to analyzing systemic racism and white privilege. The next two days explored what it means to be an antiracist ally to people of color. The final two days focused on organizational change: how historically white organizations can take specific steps toward becoming antiracist, multiracial, and multicultural. Between each of the two-day sessions, participants were assigned articles, podcasts, videos, and reflection questions related to the topics we would explore in the upcoming session. From start to finish, DOOW's focus was systemic racism and antiracist activism, but the seminar was also an intersectional learning environment where facilitators and participants grappled with multiple forms of oppression and their relationship to systemic racism.

Utilizing input from the facilitators; assigned readings by scholars, artists, and activists of color; videos; small- and large-group discussion; structured exercises; and guest presentations by colleagues of color, participants explored the following topics and issues:

- The four realms of racism: personal, interpersonal, institutional, and cultural
- Historical roots of racism in the United States
- Movements for racial justice in the United States
- White privilege and unearned advantage
- Claiming and shaping an antiracist identity
- Practicing the skills of interrupting racism
- Strategies for institutional change
- How to sustain this lifelong work
- Developing relationships of support and accountability

We designed DOOW as a highly interactive seminar, utilizing a wide variety of participatory learning modalities including large- and small-group discussion, paired sharing, viewing and discussing films, time for individual reflection and journal writing, participation in structured activities, and skill practice at interrupting racism. In every seminar, we sought to keep reflections, discussions, and strategizing grounded in real-life experiences. We stressed that DOOW was not just an informative educational experience; it was designed for white people who sought to deepen their awareness of personal, interpersonal, cultural, and institutional racism, with the goal of becoming more effective antiracist allies.

Cocreating Our Learning Community

Our goal was to create a respectful, loving, and truth-telling environment in which participants could bring their whole selves to this vitally important work. During the initial two-day segment, we talked about the kind of learning community we needed and desired, affirming that we had the capacity to create a community anchored in trust, openness, vulnerability, and affirmation of differences. The facilitators also stressed that this kind of learning community does not happen automatically. It needs to be created, nurtured, and tended. To assist in that nurturing process, the facilitators shared a list of group guidelines and asked that participants, as well as facilitators, hold the group accountable to these group norms:

- Listen carefully to each other.
- Speak from personal experience.
- Share time and space.
- Be aware of the impact our words and actions have on others as well as the intentions we bring.
- Honor confidences.
- Do not freeze people in time (allow yourself and others to make mistakes, change, and grow).
- Recognize and honor the differences we bring.
- Challenge oppressive remarks and behaviors without blaming or shaming.
- Expect and accept discomfort and unfinished business.
- Expect joy.

In many ways, DOOW participants became cocreators of the seminar as it evolved to meet changing times and respond to the needs and longings participants named. We learned, for example, that the process of claiming and embodying an antiracist identity is not just cognitive work. It is also heart and soul work. As white people awaken to the immense suffering and gaping inequities wrought by systemic racism and white supremacy, we can feel intense grief and anger about all we have not known or been told.

The six-day format provided space, time, and guidance for learning, trying on, and practicing new behaviors when confronting racism in ourselves, in others, and in the world around us. For example, it is not uncommon for those of us who are white to experience acute embarrassment or shame when we are suddenly made aware that we have harmed others with the hurtful words we have spoken, the discriminatory policies we have supported, or the callous disregard we have displayed. Especially in an antiracist seminar like DOOW, when we suddenly recognize how oblivious we have been, we can feel flushed, exposed, and humiliated even when the person who made us aware of the harm in no way sought to induce shame in us.

To feel shame, explains psychologist Gershen Kaufman, "is to feel seen in a painfully diminished sense. The self feels exposed both to itself and to anyone else present.... Contained in the experience of shame is the piercing awareness of ourselves as fundamentally deficient in some vital way as a human being."[1]

By acknowledging how common it can be to feel this kind of shame when challenged, and by promising that we would not freeze each other in time, we practiced the skills of voicing and receiving challenge, and of finding the grace and commitment to keep learning, changing, and growing in awareness. Doing Our Own Work provided a much-needed context for white people to express their grief, anger, and shame in the presence of other white people who often identify with those feelings. But we did not only hear each other's pain. We developed new antiracist muscles by enlarging the capacity to stay present and not shut down, check out, or collapse in a heap of shame-filled tears. We learned that being in community could entail expressing anger and frustration without writing each other off. We learned how to reach out and help each of us move through fear and uncertainty, grateful that others have turned toward us—not away from us—when we were afraid and consumed by self-doubt. As I heard someone say years ago, we found the strength "to open up and toughen up." And we challenged ourselves and each other to find healing through actively working with people of color and white allies to interrupt and dismantle systemic racism in our spheres of influence.

Action and Reflection

The DOOW seminars utilized an action/reflection method of learning with the goal of equipping participants to become knowledgeable and compassionate agents of structural change in their local communities. Our reflections were grounded in antiracist action, and our action was strengthened and refined by deeper reflection, study, and dialogue. This meant that participants were constantly asking how the new knowledge and skills they were acquiring could be translated into more effective antiracist action, and how their actions could be critically reflected upon, refined, corrected, sharpened, and strengthened. The action/reflection components of the seminar included:

- Reading and discussing articles by antiracist activists, scholars, novelists, and poets.

- Viewing and discussing films, videos, and documentaries created by Black, Indigenous, and other people of color.
- Participating in a sphere-of-influence working group that focused on organizational change.
- Keeping a journal of daily experiences, insights, concerns, and questions regarding racism and efforts to confront racism.
- Checking in with other DOOW participants to receive feedback, consultation, challenge, and support.
- Skill practice at interrupting interpersonal and institutional racism.

During the initial two-day segment, we discussed the dangers inherent in an all-white group. A seminar for white people, and led by white people, can implicitly normalize certain ways of confronting racism. What white people prioritize as the important issues in confronting racism may be different from what people of color might prioritize. Another danger is the reinforcement of racial insularity. Many white people live in predominantly white worlds. An all-white seminar could suggest to white people that they can be antiracist allies without being in real-life relationships with people of color.

A critical element in the design and facilitation of DOOW seminars was ongoing consultation with antiracist educators, trainers, and activists of color. One of those colleagues, Dionardo Pizaña, was a guest presenter at DOOW seminars. He shared how glad he was that this intensive work was being done by white people, and he warned us about two temptations we could fall prey to if we failed to be mindful of them: (1) We can easily reinforce racial insularity through meeting with white people only, and (2) we could leave the seminar with a missionary spirit shaped by the misguided arrogance that we now have all the answers.

Throughout the seminar, we emphasized that white people cannot become effective antiracist allies unless we are in ongoing, accountable relationships with people of color. We spoke often about the hazards of acting unilaterally, warning participants that developing antiracist strategies and agendas without being in conversation and relationship with people of color can do more harm than good. And we encouraged participants to become engaged in grassroots antiracist organizations in their communities led by Black, Indigenous, or other people of color.

DOOW's Sphere-of-Influence Working Groups

In preparation for the first two days of DOOW, participants were invited to identify a sphere of influence in their personal or professional life where they hoped to become more knowledgeable and skillful about working with others to confront racism. That sphere of influence could be a workplace, neighborhood association, worship community, or grassroots organization. Their chosen sphere of influence served as a focus and lens for the study, reflection, discussion, and skill practice they experienced in DOOW. Each month when we gathered, participants met in sphere-of-influence working groups to share experiences, dilemmas, and incidents of concern to them.

The sphere-of-influence working group was also a context in which DOOW participants critically examined whether they were in accountable relationships with colleagues of color. If they were not, they explored what the barriers seemed to be, what role they played in those barriers, how they might alter their behaviors, and what steps they could take to nurture accountable relationships in nonintrusive ways.

Skill Practice

Practicing the skills of interrupting racism became a critically important activity in DOOW seminars. Despite their initial fear of role-playing, many DOOW participants found skill practice one of the most important exercises in the DOOW seminar. We began the skill practice sessions by acknowledging the times we have failed to speak up and speak out when white friends, family members, or coworkers uttered racist remarks. We also confessed that we had fallen silent far too often in racially diverse settings, waiting for people of color to name the offense and intervene.

We found it helpful to name and examine what lay behind this white silence when racist behaviors and policies were at play: failure to recognize the offense; fear of publicly humiliating the offender; fear of jeopardizing our rank or reputation in an organization; inability to formulate an adequate response; and fear of doing more harm than good.

As we prepared to practice speaking up and interrupting racist remarks and behaviors, we discussed positive approaches to confrontation. If our objective is to open room for change rather than simply winning an argument, we agreed it would be best to engage the person in a way that is clear, yet not condescending; that builds a bridge and opens the chance of further dialogue, rather than closing the door in a gesture of self-righteousness.

Then we broke into small groups, brainstormed difficult scenarios, analyzed how racism was at work in those scenarios, and role-played strategies for creative and constructive interventions.

Spiritual Strength for the Long Haul

To sustain a lifelong commitment to racial justice requires an infusion of spirit and courage. In DOOW, we utilized music and poetry created by artists and authors committed to racial justice, and we provided a context for participants to explore the resources they needed to sustain this work. An essential component of the seminar was the opportunity for participants to reflect upon and discuss questions such as these:

- From where do we draw strength in this work when we face demoralization or weariness?
- What and where are our resources for renewal and revitalization?
- How can we stay in this struggle for the long haul?
- What most deeply grounds and inspires our commitment to antiracism work?

As preparation for the first DOOW session, we invited participants to bring a photo, book, song, or other object that symbolized a person who inspired their passion for racial justice. That person could be living or deceased, someone they knew personally or someone they had read or heard about. One by one, participants and facilitators called the names of the people who inspired their passion for justice, shared a brief description of the person, and laid their symbols on a handwoven rug, creating a bountiful collection of precious images. After sharing our symbols and stories, we reminded each other that there were people watching us, that what we do or fail to do matters profoundly.

Three months later, at the closing ritual on the final day of the seminar, we gathered around that same handwoven rug. While listening to a recording of Sweet Honey in the Rock singing, "We who believe in freedom cannot rest until it comes," we signed the certificate that each member of the seminar received. At the top of the certificate were these words of Audre Lorde:

> If you do not use the power of who you are in the service of what you say you believe, someone else will use you, and probably to my detriment ...
>
> When I dare to be powerful—to use my strength in the service of my vision, then it becomes less and less important whether I am afraid.

And in the center were these words of support and encouragement, surrounded by our signatures:

[First name], remember we are

with you as you bring your passion,

creativity, and commitment

to the work of racial justice.

6

This Is What Accountable Relationships Look Like

DIONARDO PIZAÑA AND MELANIE S. MORRISON

Dionardo Pizaña served as the diversity, equity, and inclusion specialist for Michigan State University Extension. He is a nationally recognized, highly sought-after, multicultural consultant, speaker, and trainer with more than twenty-five years' experience developing, teaching, and facilitating diversity education programs for nonprofit, governmental, and educational institutions. In developing these ideas, we are indebted to these sources: Cushing et al., Accountability and White Anti-Racist Organizing; Tochluk and Levin, "Powerful Partnerships"; Wise, "Appreciation and Accountability."

People who are targeted by systemic injustice know far more about that injustice than those who are granted unearned privileges by that same system. Therefore, antiracist practice necessitates that white people listen to, learn from, and be accountable to Black, Indigenous and other people of color as the primary source of knowledge about racism, white supremacy, white privilege, and antiracist action.

The statements presented here are gleaned from conversations we have had over the past twelve years of working together as antiracism educators. These statements have also been informed by the wisdom of other educators and organizers. We especially want to acknowledge and express gratitude to our mentor, friend, and colleague Monique Savage.

The preface was written by Dionardo Pizaña. Later, in dialogue format, we discuss what it means to develop and nurture relationships of accountability.

We share these insights as a work in progress knowing that as we continue to learn and grow, these statements will be amended and expanded.

Preface: Foundational Principles for Partnerships of Accountability

GROUNDED IN TRUST

Partnerships of accountability must be grounded in trust—both in a moment and over time. There are many individual and systemic reasons why Black, Indigenous, and other people of color may not trust white people, so it can never be assumed that trust is present or will be sustained. There must be a clear understanding that one of the by-products of racism is mistrust and that trust with one member of a racialized group does not necessarily transfer to trust from every member of that group or community. Trust can be built through individual interactions and can be strengthened as relationships deepen and grow. Trust across racial differences can also be built through equity-based actions, individual integrity, critical self-awareness, and humility. Building trust across our racial differences can provide a strong bridge to exploring how we can build trust across our other social-identity realities (e.g., gender, gender identity, class, disability, and sexual orientation).

MOVING TOWARD INTERCONNECTEDNESS AND MUTUALITY

In what ways do white people see their lives inextricably interconnected or mutually linked with Black, Indigenous, and other people of color who are part of their lives, partnerships, and communities? Racism is upheld by the white supremacy values of individualism, fear of complexity, and paternalism. These ways of being can negatively impact the ability of white people to gravitate toward connectedness, especially when the going gets tough, or when the default is "the way that we have always done things." The proclamation from white people that they "see everyone as humans" rings hollow, as day-to-day negative impacts and outcomes continue in the lives and bodies of Black, Indigenous, and other people of color. Moving toward interconnectedness and mutuality across our racial differences does not mean that we see everyone as the same. It is centered on a greater awareness and understanding that my thoughts, beliefs, and actions are of significance and should be informed and guided by racially different individuals and groups.

DEVELOPING CRITICAL AND COMPASSIONATE SELF-REFLECTION

One of the important skills that each of us can develop as we move toward partnerships of accountability across race is to build critical and compassionate self-reflection. If you are white, how often do you look internally at the ways that you may be, intentionally or unintentionally, supporting, colluding with, or upholding racism at all four levels—personal, interpersonal, institutional, and cultural? Opening oneself to critical and compassionate self-reflection, day to day, can help move white people away from initial reactions of fear, protection, judgment, and disconnection. You can begin the process of self-reflection by noticing when you are repeating unhelpful behaviors in your relationships across racial differences, or by asking for feedback on your behaviors or language, and by becoming curious instead of reactive when emotions are high. Self-reflection is not about "going inside" to avoid difficulty or hard situations or interactions; it is about building emotional resiliency to hold yourself with compassion and accountability, to seek out important feedback for growth, and to recognize that personal change can inform changes at the interpersonal, institutional, and cultural levels.

Developing and Nurturing Relationships of Accountability

DIONARDO: Accountability is not a static reality, and it is not inherently punitive. Accountability will change and evolve with increased trust, vulnerability, and the investment of time needed to better understand how power and privilege are present at the personal, interpersonal, institutional, and cultural levels.

MELANIE: As a white person in a relationship of accountability to a Black person, Indigenous person, or other person of color, I need to enter with humility, deep listening, and critical self-reflection while also showing up with agency, authentic engagement, and a willingness to bring my whole self to the relationship.

DIONARDO: Developing and nurturing relationships of accountability requires an investment of time, energy, and commitment. Black, Indigenous, and other people of color have many reasons to doubt that white people will be willing and able to show up with the consistency and commitment necessary to build authentic accountability.

MELANIE: Being accountable as an antiracist white person means moving out of white spaces into places where we are not in control. It means becoming involved in organizations and movements that are led by Black, Indigenous, and other people of color, respecting the priorities they identify as strategies for change, and sustaining our engagement over time. It means learning about the ways Black, Indigenous, and other people of color have resisted racism long before I arrived on the scene.

DIONARDO: Accountability that is authentic and life-giving cannot be one-sided communication. To assume that Black, Indigenous, and other people of color understand racism in more profound ways than white people is not the same as assuming that white people are inherently untrustworthy or less than equal partners in the accountable relationship.

MELANIE: If white people believe we are less than equal partners in accountable relationships, we will likely seek personal validation and worth from Black, Indigenous, or other people of color. And we stay stuck in guilt, suffer from a chronic sense of self-deprecation, and distrust our own deepest wisdom.

DIONARDO: Accountability cannot be one sided, because all of us have target and nontarget identities. In accountable relationships that are authentic and life-giving, both people are engaged in critical self-examination and learning from each other as we seek to understand and confront the privileges we carry.

MELANIE: Accountable relationships are mutually enriching, but they do not always result in friendship. If I enter into a relationship of accountability with a Black person, an Indigenous person, or another person of color and it develops into a friendship, that can be a wonderful gift for both of us, but there is no guarantee that developing a solid and sustainable relationship of accountability will result in friendship.

DIONARDO: As a person of color in accountable relationships with white allies and accomplices, I expect those white people to show up in solidarity alongside me. I do not expect that they will speak for me or other people of color but rather speak from their own racial experience and understandings.

MELANIE: Being in accountable relationships with Black, Indigenous, or other people of color does not mean relinquishing my critical sensibilities or ignoring my deepest wisdom. It means a willingness to consistently check in with and learn from people who are the targets of racism and have the most at stake in the struggle for racial justice—namely Black, Indigenous, and other people of color.

DIONARDO: As a person of color, I am willing to engage as an accountability partner with white people who have demonstrated through their words, actions, and persistence that they are committed to the long-haul struggle for racial equity and full inclusion. They earn my trust not because they do it perfectly, but because they continue to show up with all their imperfections and act from a stance of understanding that our lives are interconnected.

MELANIE: Being accountable as an antiracist white person means that I must listen to and learn from Black, Indigenous, and other people of color as the primary sources if I want to understand racism, white supremacy, white privilege, and antiracist practice. I can also gain knowledge and guidance about racism, white supremacy, white privilege, and antiracist practice from white people who have developed a healthy antiracist white identity and who are engaged in critical self-reflection and sustained antiracism work with Black, Indigenous, and other people of color.

DIONARDO: From a place of accountability, I trust that you care about me and understand what causes me harm well enough that you will have my back even if I am not present.

MELANIE: There will be times when I must speak and act to interrupt racism before I have the chance to check in with Black, Indigenous, and other people of color or with white allies, but accountability means that I am open to being corrected and to apologizing when my words, actions, and good intentions have caused harm.

DIONARDO AND MELANIE: Accountability has to do with developing and nurturing relationships that are authentic and life-giving for both parties. The ultimate goal of accountability is to build strong and healthy partnerships that undergird and sustain the lifelong work of dismantling systemic racism and white supremacy.

7

Dear White People

This message was posted on social media five days after the Charleston Church massacre on June 17, 2015.

Dear White People:

Difficult as it may be, you and I must listen to and grapple with the words that Dylann Roof spoke as he began shooting the people who warmly, graciously welcomed him into the Bible study circle at Emmanuel AME Church on June 17, 2015: "You are raping our women and taking over the country. You have to go."

Those words are a mirror for us as a people—as white people.

Those words are not only the isolated rantings of a tormented soul. We can't simply scratch our heads and wonder how someone could be so hate-filled. We can't only conclude that we need stricter gun control. We don't need to interview his family and friends to understand where those words came from.

The words Dylann Roof spoke are quite literally the white narrative that has undergirded and sustained systemic racism for centuries. That narrative continues unabated.

Those words represent the fears and stereotypes that undergird present day racial profiling, state sanctioned violence, and mass incarceration. Those words feed anti-immigrant hysteria. Those words ring out in the chant, "Give us our country back."

Dylann Roof's words are a mirror we must face as a people—as white people—if we are going to do the deep work required of us. None of us is exempt from this work. You and I and all of us must do this work.

Melanie S. Morrison
Executive Director, Allies for Change

II. ANCESTRAL INVESTIGATIONS

8

Cultural Envy

Collective pride, which is a form of nourishing, group self-love, is an emotional experience that many white people find elusive. —LILLIAN ROYBAL ROSE, "White Identity and Counseling White Allies About Racism," 1996

I was forty-two years old before anyone in the United States asked me to identify my ethnic and cultural background. It happened during the first evening of an antiracism training. We were invited to go around the circle and, in one minute's time, introduce ourselves by sharing something about our ethnic and cultural roots. I was enormously relieved when the leader asked a person on the other side of the room to get us started. When my turn came, I introduced myself as the daughter of two white Southerners who had moved north to attend seminary in their early twenties. To illustrate that I come from a long line of fiercely independent women, I recounted a brief anecdote about my Appalachian grandmother. I expressed gratitude for my parents, who modeled a deep and abiding passion for social justice and mentioned that while I was fairly certain my father's people came from Scotland, I had no clue about my mother's people.

That I explained my ethnic roots with such brevity was not accidental. I had no ancestral stories to share. I did not know when or under what circumstance my ancestors had emigrated to the United States or in what part of the country they had originally settled. The only inkling I had that my father's people were Scottish was the Morrison Scottish plaid and coat of arms that hung in the front entryway of our home when I was growing up. If pressed, I might have confessed an intense dislike for bagpipe music and, except for a vague desire to see Scotland's hills, I had never longed to visit the motherland.

The next time I participated in a cultural exercise proved even more challenging. It occurred during a three-day multicultural training that included twenty-four participants who had been selected with a stated concern for optimizing diversity with regard to race, age, and gender. The training was led by a Black woman whom I will call "Shirley" and by a white man whom I will name "Phil."

At the beginning of the second day, the trainers divided us into four racial/ethnic affinity groups that reflected the racial identities of the people present: African American, Asian American, Latina/o, and European American. Each affinity group was invited to discuss this question: What do you love about your culture?

We were allotted ten minutes to jot down personal responses to this question, and an additional twenty minutes to create a composite list that would later be shared in the whole group. Before giving us the green light to begin, Shirley reviewed the definition of culture: "The vast structure of behaviors, ideas, attitudes, values, habits, customs, language, rituals, ceremonies and practices peculiar to a particular group of people, and that provides them with a general design for living and with patterns for interpreting reality."[1]

When told to begin, I closed my eyes and tried to engage my heart as well as my head, reaching to recall sensory images from my childhood that might capture some of the customs, rituals, and values of my family and church community.

I could not believe ten minutes had passed when Phil called time and invited us to choose a volunteer in each affinity group to record the composite list on newsprint. A young woman named Mary agreed to serve as the recorder of our European American group, but no one seemed eager to share answers to the question, What do you love about your culture? The subdued energy resident in our group stood in sharp contrast to the spirited conversations emanating from other affinity groups. We stared at our notepads and shot sideways glances at the other groups as their shouts of delight and laughter ricocheted around the room.

"Okay, I'll start," said one brave woman in our group. "As a white person, I don't have to worry about being racially profiled."

The man next to her nodded and jumped in: "I am not followed by security guards in stores."

Like popcorn, responses burst forth in rapid succession around our table as people recited items from Peggy McIntosh's article about white privilege.[2] "I don't have to worry about thinking I got my job because of affirmative action." People were smiling now as they spoke up: "I can find Band-Aids in my skin color when I go to the store."

Glancing down at my list, it seemed suddenly out of place. I turned it over, face down. When my turn came, my heart was pounding as I said, "Maybe I misunderstood the assignment. I could swear that Phil and Shirley invited us to list the things we love about our culture."

"They did," confirmed several people at once.

"So you love not being followed by security guards?" I asked the man who had named this item.

"Well, *love* may be putting it too strongly," he shot back. "But I'm definitely happy that I don't have to face the things people of color have to contend with every day. That's what it means to be white in this culture: We have unearned privilege and power."

"That's right," another person chimed in.

Yet another person interjected, "I don't think we are supposed to be judging each others' lists. This is a brainstorming exercise. Why don't you read us your answers, Melanie?"

My cheeks and the tips of my ears were hot as I read my list aloud:

- Music filled our home. As children, my sisters and I loved to dance around the piano before bedtime while my mother played tunes from the Alan Lomax folk songbook.
- My father read poems to us by James Weldon Johnson, Dylan Thomas, and William Blake.
- My mother taught us folk dances from different parts of the world and sang us to sleep with lullabies from different countries.
- My parents often talked with profound gratitude about the people, books, and events that had awakened them, shaken them to their core, and helped them critically examine their racist conditioning.

- On our kitchen wall, next to the round table where we ate all our meals, was a huge map of the world. After meals, my sisters and I would play "I spy a country that begins with the letter..."
- Our living room was a gathering place for community groups.

Mary was still transcribing my additions when Phil called time. He invited the African American group to post their list and read it aloud to us. It took several group members to hang the four pages of newsprint filled with a wide array of things, including the wisdom and witness of their ancestors, the nurture and mentoring of young people, the importance of family, many different foods, multiple genres of music, literature, poetry, dance, family rituals, and a wide array of religious practices.

The lists shared by the Latina/o and Asian American groups were also several sheets in length. Both of these groups explained that they did not have sufficient time to record all the things they loved because so many different cultures were represented in each of their affinity groups. They challenged the artificiality of the racial designations that had lumped them together as Latina/o and Asian American. Nevertheless, they shared their lists with delight and pride. Group members called out encouragement and clapped as each item was read aloud.

Ours was the last group to report. Mary spoke so softly while reading the list that Phil asked her to speak up. She cleared her throat a couple times and started again. As the list was read, there was no audible encouragement from our group or from anywhere in the room. The laughter that had been so plentiful just moments before was replaced by somber silence. Shirley motioned to Phil that she would like to step in.

"Excuse me, Mary. I'm perplexed by the things on your list. So far, all the items you have named are what Peggy McIntosh describes as 'unearned privileges.' Are these the things that you all love about your culture?"

Mary hunched her shoulders. Her face flushed, and her voice cracked as she responded, "This is what we came up with."

"Well, this is an excellent illustration of the fact that 'white' isn't really an ethnicity," Shirley said. "White is what European Americans became when they ceased being Italian or Polish or Irish or Scottish. They traded their cultural traditions for an invented racial category that said they were superior to all other races."

Shirley paused before continuing, "And yet, it is also true that there are dominant cultural norms in this society that could be called white. We are going to discuss these later in the training."

Shirley apologized for interrupting and invited Mary to read the rest of the list. Fearing another intervention by Shirley, I held my breath as my responses were read aloud. But Mary finished, and the leaders suggested we take a break.

When the group reconvened, the leaders introduced a new activity. I did not hear the instructions because I was still processing the last exercise. Every item my affinity group had listed seemed inadequate, even pathetic, compared with the lists from the other groups. The white privileges were not really cultural attributes, and my list seemed hopelessly idiosyncratic to my family. And something Shirley mentioned when she questioned our affinity group list confused me. Had she stated that white culture is both nonexistent and dominant? How could it be both, I wondered?

My fear of appearing clueless kept me from asking about this in the plenary session. Instead, I jotted down a list of questions in the small yellow notebook that contained my daily ruminations about white privilege and racism:

- What would pride in, or love of, my culture look like, feel like, as a white person?
- Who are my people? Are all white people my people? If not, why not? And who then?
- Is it desirable or even possible to recover my ancestral roots, be they Scottish or some other ethnic heritage? What will be gained by doing so? What is lost by not doing so?
- What would it mean to love my white self, my white body, in ways that do not reek of superiority?

I have carried these questions with me for years. In the Doing Our Own Work antiracism seminars I have facilitated for white people, I heard these questions asked again and again in different ways. When asked to identify ethnicity, many participants shrugged their shoulders and admitted that they did not have a clue where their ancestors hailed from. Some gave voice to intense envy for the rich cultures their friends of color seemed to possess.

James Baldwin called it "the price of the ticket."[3] To become white in America means to forswear or mute our ethnic traditions. To anglicize names that sound too Polish, Czech, or Portuguese. To engage in practices that exclude and oppress others so that our "people" might merit the privileges associated with whiteness. Over generations, the desires and practices of assimilation can lead to ancestral ignorance.

During the twenty-six years I led Doing Our Own Work seminars, participants who could fluently articulate their ethnic and cultural roots were a distinct minority. Some were able to recall anecdotal fragments such as "Oma sang me lullabies from the Netherlands," or "Grandpa used to lapse into Italian expletives when he got mad."

Those most able to name ethnicity and culture were first- or second-generation immigrants to the United States, or people who claimed an accompanying identity that set them apart from mainstream white culture. I worked for many years cofacilitating Doing Our Own Work with Ann Flescher, a Jewish woman whose people came to the United States from Poland to escape the Nazi occupation and Holocaust. Ann was eloquent in describing how her religious and ethnic roots shaped the expressions she used, the foods she ate, the things she feared, what made her laugh, and the values she held dear.

When I facilitated with Ann, the paucity of knowledge about my ethnic roots stood in stark contrast to her cultural fluency. Unlike Ann, I was hard pressed to answer the reflection questions we developed for Doing Our Own Work participants:

In what ways were you aware of your ethnic background when you were growing up?

How is your ethnic background reflected in your current values, practices, customs, and personal priorities?

After many years of leading Doing Our Own Work seminars, I yearned for a clearing where I could give uninterrupted attention to the thorny, irascible questions about white identity, culture, pride, and ancestry that kept reappearing in those seminars. If Ann and I failed to make them part of the curriculum, they would appear regardless, like uninvited guests who, after throwing open the meeting room doors and defiantly placing their chairs in the circle, announced, "We belong here and we have no intention of leaving." We wrestled mightily with these questions in Doing Our Own Work, usually without finding consensus or closure.

If asked why I decided to take four months' sabbatical in 2008 and begin the journey into genealogical investigations, I might say, "Cultural envy made me do it." I had grown weary of hearing myself say, "These matters are exceedingly complex" when addressing questions of white identity and culture. The questions in my little yellow notebook begged for attention. It was long past time to do the deep, hard work of discovering my ancestral origins.

9

Genealogy as Spiritual Practice

REFLECTIONS ON MY WHITE
ANCESTRAL WORK

To investigate the details of our family, local and ethnic histories is to do an accounting of the debts and assets we have inherited. It is an act of spiritual and political integrity to own and acknowledge the precise nature of this inheritance.—AURORA LEVINS MORALES, *Medicine Stories*, 2019

Every time I log on to Ancestry.com, I run the risk of being swallowed whole. With each new person or generation added, multiple green leaves appear on the branches, fluttering seductively, inviting me to attach this birth certificate, that death notice, or this list of passengers aboard a ship from England. There is no end to the threads that can be followed. My original question can be lost as I fall down another rabbit hole lined with historical minutia. While on sabbatical fifteen years ago, I often stayed up most of the night, clicking on each new glittering leaf like a gambler promising herself for the seventeenth time that this will be the last roll of the dice.

I choose to take these addictive and distracting risks because there is something more than glittering leaves that compels me to log on each day. It is the search for roots: the search to know from whence I come and the search to understand more deeply who my people are. That search is embedded in another lifelong quest born of legacy and personal commitment: namely, to understand both what it means to be white in these United States of America and the consequent responsibilities for repairing the breaches that white supremacy has created. My family's genealogy is inevitably a racial genealogy because this nation, from the moment Europeans invaded its shores, has been inextricably bound up with the construction and reconstruction of racial identities intended to privilege some and exploit or annihilate others.

I am driven to understand my racial, cultural, and ethnic roots as something more than an interesting historical exercise. I have witnessed so often how those of us who are white deny that we are "raced"—proudly asserting that we are simply human or American. We bemoan that we do not have a culture and seek to fill this void by mimicking the cultural identities and practices of others. I am compelled to understand my people's histories more precisely and deeply because people of color have said to me, "I appreciate that you want to understand my culture and history as a person of color in this country. But you need to do some deep investigation of your own cultural history and experience. You need to do the hard and strenuous work of understanding what it means to be white in America."

I do not want to study my ancestors in a historical vacuum. I want to understand who they were and the choices they faced by studying the economic, political, and social forces at work in the communities and regions in which they lived. Every community—from the tiniest village to the largest metropolitan area—contains histories of oppression and resistance that call to be mined, shared, and archived. Every community has stories of people who resisted oppression by organizing, harboring fugitives, speaking up and speaking out, writing editorials, engaging in sit-down strikes, loving, befriending, and marrying across race and class lines, writing poetry, preaching sermons, and singing songs of protest and pride. Every community also contains stories of people who colluded with systems that promised privilege, exploited others, failed to speak out, betrayed family members in the quest for wealth, turned their backs on the plight of neighbors, or actively engaged in racial violence.

We need to recover the stories of our ancestors to understand the choices they made in relation to systems of privilege and oppression. Who they are and what we inherited from them by way of debts or assets should inform the work each of us is called to do as we seek to confront and dismantle the contemporary manifestations of white supremacy and racism. Some of our ancestors may be people whose spirits we can call upon in times of trial, demoralization, or despair. Other ancestors may inspire our work as we seek to embody a retributive justice that repays in some measure what those ancestors stole from their contemporaries.

Unless those of us who are white grasp the historical and cultural specifics of how racism has shaped our lives, I fear our work on behalf of racial justice will be sporadic at best. Genealogy by itself will not provide this understanding or generate a passion for justice. But genealogy done in the context of antiracist activism can provide one means of grounding, orienting, and sustaining us in work that is never done once and for all.

In her book *Medicine Stories: Essays for Radicals*, Aurora Levins Morales, a Puerto Rican Jewish writer and poet, tells how she grew up hearing stories from her mother about the racism and economic exploitation she faced as a Puerto Rican child in the barrios of Spanish Harlem during the Great Depression. But then, "It was not until I went to the small Puerto Rican town of Tao Alta," explains Morales, "and examined the parish registers that I discovered five generations of slaveholding ancestors among the local landed gentry of northeastern Puerto Rico."[1]

Far from burying herself in grief and shame, Morales asked how these familial roots could deepen and expand her work as an activist. The discovery of enslaving ancestors in her mother's lineage has given her a greater sense of connection and compassion for others who bear an enslaving past. It has also emboldened her hope that a privileged legacy can be altered and transformed. In my genealogical investigations, I have learned that something as commonplace as a photograph, a letter, or the fragment of a family story can serve as the key to unlock the first door into radical genealogy.

In my case, it was a seemingly innocent question regarding the origin of my grandfather's name, Truman Aldrich Morrison, that unearthed my family's connection to the convict lease system in Birmingham, Alabama. The mystery was solved when I came upon an article about Truman Hemenway Aldrich that appeared in the August 19, 1928, edition of the *Birmingham News*. After the Civil War, Truman Aldrich convinced his brother-in-law, George Morrison, to combine their financial assets and move from New Jersey to Alabama. A mining and civil engineer by training, Aldrich began prospecting the coalfields near Birmingham. He became one of the wealthiest coal magnates in the history of Alabama and an industrial founder of Birmingham.

In 1884, Truman Aldrich recruited his wife's nephew, John Morrison—my great-grandfather—to serve as a supervisor in a new mining community he was developing. Holding his uncle in high esteem, my great-grandfather named his firstborn child Truman Aldrich Morrison. A generation later, my father was named Truman Aldrich Morrison Jr.

In my research, I learned of Truman Aldrich's mining practices and the convict lease system that reenslaved thousands of Black men during the decades following emancipation. Using laws enacted to intimidate newly freed Black people, law enforcement officials throughout Alabama arrested Black men, the courts charged inflated bail that could not be paid by the defendants, and these men were held in prison. Officials collected revenues by leasing prisoners to the owners of mines, railroads, lumber camps, and farms.

The convict lease system was not outlawed in Alabama until 1928, and it served as a major source of revenue for state and county budgets struggling in the wake of war and emancipation.

I often name my father, Truman Aldrich Morrison Jr., when I attend antiracism trainings and I am asked to name someone who has inspired my commitment to racial justice. My passion for racial justice and my work as an antiracism educator were seeded by the stories my father told and the lifelong activism he modeled.

Through my genealogical practice, I have come to understand more deeply that I have also inherited class and race privileges that have spelled deprivation and degradation for others. Having opened the doors that led me to uncover the convict lease system and so much more, I cannot say my father's name or mine without also bringing that legacy into the room.

Genealogy becomes a form of spiritual practice as I acknowledge the complex and often contradictory inheritance from my ancestors, and as I remember that what I do and fail to do will impact those who come after me. Recognizing the debts and the assets of what I have inherited emboldens me to bring a heightened sense of self-scrutiny and accountability to my own life and activism, asking: What have I done with what has been given me? What will I leave for those who come after me?

10

Why We Must Remember

A KING DESCENDANT'S RECKONING WITH
HER ENSLAVING ANCESTORS

*Keynote address, April 14, 2022, at a University of Montevallo conference,
"Why We Must Remember: A King House and Africatown Event."*

In 2008, two years after my father's death, I was having lunch with my Aunt Harriet in Raleigh, North Carolina, when she excused herself from the table, saying she needed to find something very important to show me. I thought perhaps she had gone to search for a favorite photograph of my father from their childhood years in Birmingham. When she returned, she was carrying a thin burgundy book with gold lettering on the cover. She stroked the title as she read it aloud: *The Lives and Times of Kingswood in Alabama, 1817-1890.*[1]

"Melanie," she said, "this is a book about an elegant historic mansion they used to call Kingswood. Now it's known as King House. It was the home of our ancestors in Montevallo, Alabama."

Aunt Harriet opened the cover and pointed to the author's personal inscription on the first page: "To Harriet Poole, with kindest regards and best wishes, Golda W. Johnson."

Golda Johnson was the wife of Kermit Johnson, president of the University of Montevallo in the 1970s. There was a handwritten letter from Ms. Johnson taped on the next page, and Harriet read portions of the letter aloud before ceremoniously relinquishing her prized possession.

"I want you to have this book. Did your father ever tell you that you are a descendant of Edmund King, a wealthy landowner who did much to develop the town of Montevallo?"

I shook my head. I had never heard mention of Edmund King or Montevallo.

"Your great-aunt Bessie Morrison Mussey worked closely with Golda Johnson in the renovation of King House a few decades ago," Harriet continued. "Aunt Bessie ran an antique shop in Mountain Brook. She took a keen interest in refurbishing King House because her mother, Marie Shortridge Morrison, was born in that house in 1867. Did your father ever tell you that his grandmother was born in Montevallo?"

"No," I replied again.

The name Marie Shortridge Morrison was as unfamiliar to me as the name Edmund King. I had no memory of my father ever mentioning his grandparents.

I had long known that my father was profoundly estranged from his father. In high school, my father began to question Birmingham's Jim Crow racism, from which his family materially benefited in countless ways. Whenever he voiced his growing belief that segregation was morally bankrupt and socially unjust, his father reacted with rage, and his mother changed the subject.

Inspired to pursue the ministry and a call to racial justice work, my father left Birmingham in 1940 to attend seminary in Chicago. When my father left the South, my grandfather considered him a three-time traitor, betraying his class, his region, and his race. This estrangement between father and son is one of the reasons I only met my grandfather twice before he died at age eighty-four. But sitting there with Aunt Harriet, I had to wonder, was it true that my father had never spoken of his grandparents? Or had I forgotten their names? If he had never spoken of them, was he hiding something from me and my siblings?

Thrown off balance by this sudden rush of questions, I nevertheless received the book about King House and our ancestors from Aunt Harriet as a mantle handed down to me from a family elder.

Her gift piqued my interest in the King family, so I began some preliminary research about these ancestors when I returned home to Michigan. I learned that Edmund King was part of the westward migration of white enslavers from Virginia and Georgia that took place in the wake of the Creek Wars in 1813–14. Wealthy landowners like King saw great promise in the millions of acres that had been newly seized by the US government. In 1817, Edmund King and his wife, Nancy, brought their two small children and fifteen enslaved people to what would become Montevallo, Alabama.

The narratives I found in this first round of cursory research stated that the King family made their journey in a family carriage with two covered wagons that carried their possessions. A Muscogee leader named William Weatherford (also known as Chief Red Eagle) rode with them on horseback for much of the journey, providing safe escort for King and his family through Muscogee-occupied territories.[2]

This recurring description of the King family's journey from Georgia to Alabama raised numerous questions that I longed to investigate when time permitted. There was no mention of wagons to carry the enslaved. Were they shackled in coffles as they walked more than two hundred miles from Griffin, Georgia, to Montevallo? How many Black children and elders made that journey on foot? How many had to endure the trauma of forced separation from family members left behind in Georgia? How and when did Edmund King and William Weatherford meet? Why would Weatherford provide protection for King, a white settler who was coming to occupy land in Muscogee territory?[3]

During that online search, I discovered that King House is widely considered a haunted house. Several ghost stories have circulated through the decades, most revolving around Edmund King and his considerable wealth.[4] According to campus legend, the ghost of King has been spotted in an upstairs bedroom seated at a table counting his money. Some insist that they have witnessed a shadowy figure late at night carrying a lantern near the King family cemetery that lies a few hundred feet from King House. It is believed that he buried gold in a peach orchard that used to stand near the cemetery. For years, the university, the Chamber of Commerce, and the Montevallo Arts Council sponsored a Ghost Walk in late October that included a visit to King House.

After that initial flurry of online searches, I had to put the King family research on hold because my work as director of Allies for Change was demanding, and I was immersed in researching and writing *Murder on Shades Mountain*.[5]

Eight years passed before the King family came into my purview again, through a rather uncanny convergence of events. Desperate to finish a rough draft of *Murder on Shades Mountain* in the spring of 2016, I was searching for an apartment or house near the Birmingham archives where I could hunker down and write with abandon for ten weeks. A Birmingham friend called, her voice trembling with excitement.

"I've found a house for you," she said. "It's a perfect place for writing. At the edge of town, on a large, wooded lot. My friends will be out of town for three months. They need a house sitter to care for their thirteen-year-old border collie."

The timeline meshed perfectly with mine. There was only one drawback: The house was in Montevallo.

I hesitated before accepting this offer. The distance from the Birmingham archives was inconsequential; it was the proximity to King House that worried me. To be living for ten weeks so close to King House felt intriguing, a bit ominous, and not entirely coincidental.

Fearing I would be thrown off-center and distracted from finishing my rough draft of *Murder on Shades Mountain*, I waited until the ninth week in Montevallo to call the university and make an appointment to see King House.

First Visit to the King House

As I approached King House on that first visit, I was wondering, Why do I feel compelled to visit this ancestral home? Yes, I am a descendant of Edmund King, but I have many great-great-great-great-grandfathers who hail from different parts of the country.

And then... I walked into the King House parlor and saw the portrait of Bessie Morrison Mussey, my father's aunt, that hangs on the wall opposite the painting of Edmund King. Bessie Mussey is the woman who worked with Golda Johnson during the renovation of King House in the 1970s.

I only met Aunt Bessie once in my life. I was thirteen years old, but I retain a vivid memory of her. On a family trip to Alabama, she hosted us on her veranda in Helena, wearing a large straw hat, serving us tall glasses of iced tea, and regaling us with family stories. My father always spoke of his Aunt Bessie as a "force to contend with," and that portrait in King House mirrors this description. Bessie is seated with a dalmatian dog to her left, smiling ever so slightly, wearing an elegant lime-colored evening gown and an elbow-length chiffon jacket.

Finding Aunt Bessie's portrait was tangible confirmation that I was in some primal way connected to that house. Gazing at her portrait, I was once again visited by questions about my father. Why had he never spoken about this house or Montevallo? That silence was so at odds with the man I had known since birth.

After I inspected every room in King House, my guide asked if I wanted to visit the family cemetery.

"If you have time to take me there, I would be grateful," I replied.

"Yes, of course, I have time," she said, motioning toward the back door. "It would be my pleasure to do so."

The King family cemetery is lodged between two university buildings. A rough-hewn limestone wall surrounds the cemetery. Within those walls are several trees and the gravestones of twelve family members, including Edmund King, who died in 1863.

I was grateful that I was allowed entrance to this cemetery, but once inside I felt more like an intruder than a member of the family. I had no emotional attachment to any of the people buried there. I did not bring a bouquet of flowers to lay in reverent remembrance. I would have been hard pressed to describe most of them by any physical features. I stood reading and rereading the inscription on Edmund King's gravestone—a white stone obelisk—trying to conjure images of the man it described:

> EDMUND KING
> born in Va.
> removed to Ga. And
> married Nancy Ragan
> in 1812, came to Alabama in
> 1817 and settled in this
> place where he died
> June 28, 1863,
> in the 82nd year of his life.
> *He was a wise and just*
> *man, a kind neighbor, a*
> *patriotic citizen, and was*
> *for more than fifty years*
> *an earnest and consistent*
> *member of the Baptist*
> *Church.*

What do these people mean to me? I wondered. *What significance do King House and this cemetery have for my life so many generations removed?*

As I closed the cemetery's iron gate behind me, I asked my guide if there was another cemetery on this former plantation land where enslaved people were buried.

"No, there isn't any cemetery that we know of," she replied.

Unable to fathom what she was saying to me, I asked one more time.

"Where are the enslaved people buried; the people who built King House?"

Without saying anything, she motioned to the land.

I stood there by the gate, not moving, unable to speak. Could it be that the bodies of Black men, women, and children are lying in unmarked graves on this campus, perhaps under buildings, redbrick roads, and parking lots?

Returning home to Michigan, I couldn't shake the thought that King descendants had a place to go to pay respects to their ancestors, but descendants of the people who worked for decades on that land and in King House did not have a comparable place to grieve and celebrate their beloved ancestors.

A Haunted House

When I first read about the ghost sightings at King House, I waved aside those testimonies as colorful folklore, but the more I have studied the meaning of ghosts in African American cultural traditions and their role in the novels of African American writers such as Nobel laureate Toni Morrison, I have come to believe that King House ghosts could be messengers calling us to a collective reckoning with the history of slavery on this land.[6]

In her novel *Beloved*, Toni Morrison describes the legacies of slavery as personal and collective trauma that must be faced if we are to move forward as a nation. Reflecting on the writing of *Beloved*, Toni Morrison said, "When finally I understood the nature of a haunting—how it is both what we yearn for and what we fear, I was able to see the traces of a ghostly presence, the residue of a repressed past."[7]

And speaking of ghosts, Morrison said, "I think of ghosts and haunting as just being alert. If you are really alert then you see the life that exists beyond the life that is on top. It's not spooky necessarily, might be, but it doesn't have to be. It's something I relish rather than run from."[8]

I have been to this campus five times in the past six years. During each visit, I experienced something akin to a ghostly presence, something taking me deeper each time into my own ancestral connections to King House and beckoning me to investigate the residues of a repressed past that lies below the surface.

The First White Child

I had my first glimmer of this ghostly presence while doing research about the King family on Ancestry.com. As I constructed a family tree, I learned that I was connected to the King family through Edmund King's daughter, Elizabeth, who was born in 1817, shortly after the King family arrived in what became Montevallo.

Because of my direct lineage to her, I compiled a brief sketch of Elizabeth that I hoped I might someday research more closely. I noted that she was eighteen when she married George Shortridge, also of Montevallo. He was an enslaver and circuit judge who ran for governor of Alabama in 1855 and served as the Shelby County delegate to the Secessionist Convention in 1860. When Edmund King became a widower and his health began to wane, Elizabeth moved back to King House in 1860 to care for her father. She remained there during the Civil War when the men of her family left to fight for the Confederacy. When Edmund King died in 1863, King House was left to Elizabeth and George Shortridge. They lived there until 1870, when George died and Elizabeth left Montevallo to live with her daughter in Austin, Texas.

But there was something else I learned about Elizabeth in that preliminary research that made a deep impression on me. A very brief description of her on the university website stated, "Before the end of the year that brought the [King] family from Georgia, a third child named Elizabeth was born. Legend holds that she was the first white child to be born in the community that later became Montevallo."

I stared at those words—*the first white child born in Montevallo*. Counting on my fingers, I calculated that she was my great-great-great-grandmother. Hardly breathing, I tried to fathom all that was bestowed on Elizabeth with that so-called honorific title and all the Muscogee history that was simultaneously rendered invisible.

That local legend proclaimed that Montevallo's history began with the birth of a white child. I couldn't help wondering how Elizabeth wore that legendary status in subsequent years and how her understanding of what it meant to be a white woman was passed down to her daughters and granddaughters, including Marie Shortridge Morrison, my great-grandmother.

The other group of people rendered invisible in this declaration about Elizabeth's birth were the enslaved Africans who were forced to make Montevallo their new home when the Kings settled there. Those men, women, and children are a crucial part of Montevallo's origin, but in the dominant narratives they remain unnamed more than two hundred years after Montevallo's founding. Nowhere in the histories of Montevallo I have found do we read the name of the first Black child born in Montevallo.

Later, when I returned to Montevallo and decided to devote time and energy to learning more about the King and Shortridge families, I wondered if I was making too much of this appellation, investing it with too much meaning. But then I found Elizabeth King Shortridge's obituary, published after she died in January 1906. In this lengthy tribute, she was lauded as an "aged lady" whose life and family were intimately woven with the history of her hometown. And the second sentence of that obituary declared Elizabeth King Shortridge was known as the first white child born in Montevallo.[9]

That reference to her birth in 1817 wasn't just a celebration of a long life well lived. It heralded the triumph of whiteness. Her birth was proclaimed as the dawning of a new era in that region of Alabama, as the Muscogee people were forcibly dispossessed and white planters like Edmund King staked their claim.

That legendary status was no trifling matter. Did Elizabeth wear it as a badge of honor in every stage of her life? Did it become more important to her and some other white people in Montevallo after the Civil War, as a tangible remnant of the glory days they cherished as a Lost Cause?

Some of Elizabeth's descendants have worn this badge proudly. That became clear to me when I discovered my great-grandmother's obituary in the *Birmingham News*. Marie Shortridge Morrison was seventy-five years old when she died in 1942. Although she had lived for forty-three years in Birmingham, her obituary hearkened back to her birth in Montevallo and to her own grandmother, who "was said to be the first white child born in Shelby County."[10]

After hearing me reflect on this, a friend here in Montevallo warned me, "You know, Melanie, if you keep returning to Montevallo, talking about King House and the untold stories it holds, you might become known as the great-great-great-granddaughter of the first white person born in Montevallo."

My friend was being facetious, but I took those words to heart.

I do not want to die being heralded as the great-great-great-granddaughter of the first white person born in Montevallo. I do want to live, reckoning with what it means to be a descendant of Elizabeth King Shortridge. I want to work with others to tell a fuller, truer story about my ancestors, and I want to be engaged in acts of repair for the egregious history of slavery and the inequities it created in its wake.

My third trip to Montevallo was in 2019. I was on campus four days as the Hallie Farmer lecturer. On the last afternoon, I met in the King House parlor with a small group of faculty, staff, and community residents who had been invited to talk with me about the history of King House and the people enslaved by the King and Shortridge families. After that week on campus and that conversation in the King House parlor, I knew that I had to clear space in my vocational life to make research and writing about the King and Shortridge families a priority.

I also knew that I couldn't do this work in isolation. I needed the support, challenge, wisdom, and accountability of people here in Montevallo as well as friends and colleagues in different parts of the country who bring a diversity of perspectives, life experience, and knowledge. I am deeply grateful to the people who have been journeying with me for the past three years. I had hoped to spend six weeks in Montevallo in the fall of 2020. That was prevented by COVID, but I am grateful that Zoom, emails, and phone calls sustained and deepened connections with people here.

Edmund King's Wealth

In articles and books that speak of Edmund King's role as a founding resident of Montevallo, he is lauded as a brilliant entrepreneur, a talented businessman, a successful planter, a devout Baptist, and a generous benefactor to the city.[11]

Undoubtedly, it is this that made my Aunt Harriet speak with such pride as she handed me *The Lives and Times of Kingswood*. Edmund King worked very hard as a planter, merchant, and entrepreneur who owned an iron works company; invested in a Bibb County, Alabama, cotton mill; contributed a significant amount of money to help build the Alabama and Tennessee River railroad; and donated land for the First Baptist Church.[12]

And yet these facts are only part of the story. Residues of a repressed past that lie below the surface inform us that Edmund King is one of the elite Southern planters who benefited mightily from the violent dispossession of Native people from their homelands and the enslavement of African Americans.

The military campaigns of General Andrew Jackson forced the Muscogee Nation to cede 22 million acres of land to the US government in 1814.[13] Edmund King was well aware of this when he chose this region as his new home in 1817. Between 1823 and 1828, King purchased at government auctions thousands of acres of that Muscogee land in Shelby, Bibb, and Chilton counties.[14] After Congress passed President Andrew Jackson's Indian Removal Act in 1830, forcing Muscogee, Cherokee, Choctaw, and Chickasaw peoples onto trails of tears headed west, Edmund King acquired another 9,600 acres in eight Alabama counties (Shelby, Talladega, Chilton, Bibb, Pickens, Sumter, Clay, and St. Clair).[15]

I don't know for certain what King did with all that land. I have found no evidence that he owned and managed plantations in those counties. He may have resold the land for a handsome profit as other enslavers were migrating into the state. Historian Claudio Saunt has noted that "over the course of the 1830s, the enslaved population in Alabama more than doubled to 253,000. By the end of the decade, nearly one out of every four slaves worked on land that only a few years earlier had belonged to the Creeks."[16]

It is well known that Edmund King arrived in Shelby County with fifteen enslaved people that he inherited as property when his father died in 1817. Less often cited is the fact that by 1830, King held forty-nine enslaved people in bondage. More than one-third were children under ten years of age, overwhelmingly girls.[17]

Edmund King's wealth and success can, in part, be attributed to his talent as an entrepreneur and planter, but it was the ownership of human beings that constituted the largest portion of his wealth. In the antebellum South, enslaved people became a form of property more highly valued than the cotton they harvested or the land on which they labored. As historian Steven Deyle has noted, enslaved people constituted the backbone of the Lower South's credit system: "Most owners worked their slaves not just physically but also financially, mortgaging their human property to acquire even more capital."[18]

When enslavers like Edmund King wanted to acquire more land, livestock, machinery, or slaves, they used the enslaved people they already owned as collateral. And when they could not pay creditors the money they owed, selling enslaved people was their means of paying the debt. This practice of mortgaging slaves had a devastating impact on enslaved people because it significantly increased the risk that families would be torn asunder.[19]

To better understand the historical context of my King ancestors, I have read numerous articles and books about the antebellum South, enslavement, the Civil War, the roles that white slaveholding women assumed during the Civil War, and the myriad ways Black women and men resisted enslavement and sought to care for their families, their communities, and themselves.

I have searched to no avail for diaries, letters, or other personal papers written by Edmund King or his wife, Nancy. When I told my economist friend, Robert Williams, that I had been unable to find those kinds of papers, he urged me to contact the state archivists in Montgomery to see if they might have King's will and estate papers on microfilm.

"You can learn a great deal from reading the wills and estate papers of Southern planters like Edmund King," Robert said.

Robert warned me that reading estate papers can be both tedious and excruciating. Tedious because planters were scrupulous in their record keeping, and every material object was assessed and given monetary valuation in estate papers. Every candle snuffer, razor, bedstead, curtain, buggy, mule, ox, and cow. Excruciating because the enslaved human beings who were treated as property were also assessed and given a monetary valuation.

"You will need support," Robert said. "Nothing could have prepared me for seeing the names of the men, women, and children my ancestors had held captive and exploited."

"There are names?" I asked.

I had pored over census records that enumerated the age and gender of the people enslaved by Edmund King between 1820 and 1860, but they were never identified by name.

"Yes, there are names," Robert replied. "But only first names. That, too, is very challenging. And it is enraging to realize how confounding this must be for Black people who are searching for kin."

I ordered copies of Edmund King's will and estate papers from the state archives in January 2019. They arrived while I was on the University of Montevallo campus for four days as the Hallie Farmer lecturer in March of that year. The thick manila envelope lay waiting for me on the dining room table when I returned home. I could not bear to open it right away.[20]

Later that night, my spouse, April, and I sat together with the will and estate papers spread out before us. We struggled to read the handwriting. The original ledger pages had been shrunk to make photocopies. I held onto April. My stomach tightened as we turned each page.

They revealed that Edmund King had no debt, but pieces of the land and other property were being sold to provide an ample inheritance for his surviving sons and daughters. To ensure equal distribution, every item of personal property was listed and materially assessed.[21]

The list felt endless as April read each item aloud:

2 quilts & 3 table covers $23.00, 4 spinning wheels $49.50, 1 blanket $31.00, 19 window curtains $200.00, 15 towels $22.25, 2 glass candle sticks $5.00, 3 tin pans $28.00, 1 carding machine $50.00, 5 bedsteads $225.50, 2 griddles and 2 ovens $350.00 4 shutters $56.00, 2 boxes $17.75.

April stopped reading and turned the papers face down on the table.

"I don't know if I should keep reading," she said.

"Why? What happened?" I asked, taking her hand.

"After '2 ovens, 4 shutters, and 2 boxes,' suddenly these words appeared—'29 Negroes as follows,'" April said.

"There was no line break," she continued. "No new paragraph. No heading to differentiate human beings from candlesticks. Do you want me to keep going?"

"If you can," I said, wincing, and clutching her hand. "Or should we wait?"

"There will never be a time when this will be easy," April said.

She let go of my hand, picked up the papers, gripped them with both hands, and continued reading.

"'29 Negroes as follows. Sold Lucy to P. G. King $1860.00, Minerva to Mrs. Elizabeth K. Shortridge $2550.00, Sold Julia and her youngest children Easter Ella and Georgiana to Shelby King $4000.00.'"

"Wait," I said, grabbing hold of April's arm. "Her three youngest children?"

"Yes," April replied, slowly repeating their names. "Easter. Ella. Georgiana."

"That means Julia's older children were sold to someone else," I said.

This kept happening. There were names that suggested family members were being separated and sold to different heirs, some of whom would take them to other parts of the state and country.

Why We Must Remember   71

Edmund King's death brought grief to his children and friends, but it was likely a time of terror as well as grief for the Black people he enslaved, as they anticipated their families being ripped apart, children separated from their mothers and fathers, sisters, and brothers.[22]

This rupture of Black families happened through the years as Edmund King bought and sold human beings.[23] The number of women, men, and children that Edmund King held in bondage declined significantly during the 1840s, perhaps because that was the decade in which three of King's sons reached the age of twenty-one. Having finished their university studies and travel abroad, each son may have been given enslaved people as a portion of his inheritance. It may very well have been the gift of those enslaved people that enabled William, Tom, and Peyton King to go to Louisiana, buy land in new parishes there, and start their own slave labor camps—similar to how Edmund had been able to leave Georgia, purchase land, and start new businesses in Montevallo.

Restorative Remembering, Truth Telling, and Reckoning

I don't know if there is buried gold to be found near the King House cemetery, but I do know there are countless stories in and around King House to be unearthed and critically important history to be retrieved and studied.

To assist us in this unearthing and retrieval, we fortunately have the groundbreaking work of contemporary historians such as Tiya Miles, who won the National Book Award for *All That She Carried: The Story of Ashley's Sack, a Black Family Keepsake*. With vivid detail and exquisite research, Miles recounts an intergenerational story that testifies to the creativity and tenacity of enslaved people who worked to preserve family ties.

Closer to Freedom, by historian Stephanie Camp, documents the ways that enslaved people carried out acts of everyday resistance in plantation households such as King House and created spaces in outbuildings, woods, swamps, and neighboring farms where enslaved people enjoyed moments free from white inspection, oversight, and control; spaces where they enjoyed creative expression, rest and recreation, networking, and community celebrations.[24]

And we have the writing of Joy Harjo of the Muscogee Nation, who served as the US Poet Laureate 2019-22. Harjo is a descendant of Chief Menawa, who fought General Andrew Jackson's expansion into Alabama. Harjo writes about the violence, trauma, and exile her people suffered.[25]

These are just a few of the resources we can access as we dig into archives, unearth buried stories, learn from oral histories, and bring new light to corners of darkened historical records that need illumination.

Since its sale to the Alabama Girls' Industrial School in 1908, King House has served as an infirmary, an office building, classrooms, and a guest house for visitors to the university. In recent years, there has been talk about King House becoming a research and study center. As a descendant of the King and Shortridge families, that idea makes my heart sing.

How exciting it would be for King House to become a learning space where students, faculty, staff, community members, descendants of enslaved people, and descendants of enslavers could gather to learn more about the histories and cultures of the Muscogee people; the lives and craftsmanship of the enslaved people who built King House; the spiritual practices, family traditions, and community celebrations that sustained enslaved people during their decades of bondage and brutal enslavement; and the existential crises Black people faced after emancipation when the hope of reconstruction and repair was met by white supremacist backlash and Jim Crow repression.

How exciting it would be if the University of Montevallo became the third university in Alabama to join Universities Studying Slavery—a nationwide consortium of colleges and universities that was launched by the University of Virginia in 2014.[26]

Despite the efforts by some in our nation to restrict the study of slavery and its continuing legacies, I believe there is a deep yearning in this nation for remembering, truth telling, and reckoning with the brutality of enslavement and what journalist and author Nikole Hannah-Jones calls "the audacious resilience and resistance of Black Americans."[27] I see that yearning in the profusion of art, literature, theater, film, poetry, scholarship, memorials, exhibits, and activism that call us to confront past and present racial inequities. I have heard that yearning in the work that I and my Allies for Change colleagues have done in schools where young people of all races are hankering to have honest discussions about subjects that matter, including slavery and its legacies of racial inequality. The Montevallo Community Remembrance Project is a local expression of what that restorative remembering can mean and what it can yield.[28]

Remembering and reckoning with the legacies of slavery can be hard, gut-wrenching, even excruciating, but I don't believe it is ultimately divisive work that results in useless guilt or self-loathing. Quite the contrary. I believe it is life-giving work. It is an invitation to love ourselves, others, and our country enough to do the deep work of truth telling and healing so that together we might repair the breaches that racism creates. It is an invitation to break the silences and rebuild the foundations of our communities.

11

A Just Reckoning

FORGING DEEPER,
TRUER KING HOUSE NARRATIVES

This lecture was delivered at the University of Montevallo on September 14, 2023. The lecture was co-sponsored by the Peace and Justice Studies program and the Montevallo branch of the American Association of University Women (AAUW).

I want to begin with gratitude. I am deeply grateful to the AAUW and Peace and Justice Studies for bringing us together in this two hundredth anniversary year of the building of King House, to explore what it means to forge deeper, truer narratives about what happened in that house and on the land surrounding it; the land on which we gather today.

I am grateful that we are gathered for this conversation at this moment in our nation's history—as state legislatures and local school boards north, south, east, and west seek to restrict, cancel, or ban classes and literature that dare to speak truths about the history of Indigenous dispossession and enslavement.

I am grateful that we have gathered to explore why those histories must become and remain core interdisciplinary subjects taught at every level of American education. It is my conviction that there is no one too young or too old to learn about this history in age-appropriate ways. As Clint Smith, author of *How the Word Is Passed*, stated, "The history of slavery is the history of the United States. It was not peripheral to our founding; it was central to it. It is not irrelevant to our contemporary society; it created it. This history is in our soil, it is in our policies, and it must, too, be in our memories."[1]

I am profoundly grateful for the people I have come to know in Montevallo who are working to forge deeper, truer King House narratives. Four and a half years ago, I resolved to clear space in my vocational life and make research and writing about the Kings and Shortridges of Alabama—my enslaving ancestors—a priority. I have made numerous trips to Montevallo in the past four years to walk the land, to spend time in King House and the King cemetery, to work in the Shelby County Archives, to meet with local historians, to speak on campus, and to learn from and with faculty, staff, students, and community members who are passionate about this work.

Fifty years ago, Golda Johnson wrote a book about King House and its white inhabitants titled *The Lives and Times of Kingswood in Alabama, 1817 to 1890*. Perhaps because it is the only book written specifically about King House history, it has gained a canonical status in Montevallo. Golda Johnson did extensive genealogical investigation about the King family and King descendants, and she produced a portrait of Edmund King that is often cited in articles about Montevallo's history.

In *The Lives and Times of Kingswood*, the King family is heralded as "illustrious," and Edmund King is lauded as a brilliant entrepreneur, a talented businessman, a successful planter, a devout Baptist, and a very generous benefactor to the town.[2] Undoubtedly, Edmund King worked very hard as a planter, a merchant, and an ambitious entrepreneur who owned an iron works company, invested in a Bibb County cotton mill, contributed a significant amount of money to help build the Alabama and Tennessee River railroad, and donated land for the First Baptist Church.[3]

Yet these facts are only part of the story. Edmund King could have done none of those things without the people he held in bondage for at least two generations on this land.

The people who actually built King House, and who labored for no recompense on King land, in King House, and in every industry Edmund King founded, are mentioned only five times in Golda Johnson's ninety-six-page book.[4] Only three times in those accounts did Johnson use the word "slaves." She preferred the phrase "faithful and devoted servants," implying that they loved their working conditions and remained enslaved by choice.

In her second chapter, Johnson informs the reader that Edmund King arrived in Shelby County with fifteen slaves that he inherited as property when his father died in 1817. What she fails to mention is that by 1830 (just thirteen years later), King held forty-nine people in bondage.[5] Nowhere in *The Lives and Times of Kingswood* does Johnson speak of the exploitation, dehumanization, and brutality inherent in slavery. Quite the contrary, she declares, "Slavery was a way of life. Many slaves were contented, if not happy. Some became as close to the master as other members of the household."[6]

I am grateful for the genealogical records Golda Johnson provides. But it is time for deeper, truer King House narratives to be unearthed, written, shared, and taught. I am grateful for the people on this campus and in the wider community who are passionate about forging those narratives. It has been exhilarating to participate in a mutual exchange of discoveries and sources with those engaged in this vitally important work.

It is in that collaborative spirit that I want to offer some reflections on three realms of investigation that I believe are critically important in this work of forging deeper, truer King House narratives. And I want to share some discoveries I have made related to those three realms of investigation.

The Systematic Assault on the Muscogee Nation

The first realm of investigation that deserves our never-ending attention is the blood-drenched history of how the Muscogee people were violently driven from their homelands. King House narratives must acknowledge and illuminate the profound connection between the history of Indigenous dispossession and the history of enslavement. Edmund King was part of the westward expansion by white enslavers that began in the late 1700s and early 1800s when they sought new and more fertile land on which to grow cotton and other crops. That expansion was made possible in part through the military campaigns of General Andrew Jackson.

After the Battle of Horseshoe Bend in east-central Alabama, in which Jackson's troops killed nine hundred Muscogee warriors, the Muscogee Nation was forced to cede 22 million acres of land to the US government in 1814.[7] Also, in the wake of Horseshoe Bend, Jackson sent five hundred troops into the Cahaba Valley in central Alabama to secure the territory and kill the remaining insurgent Muscogee. Many of Jackson's troops found the Cahaba Valley landscape so fertile and enticing that they returned to claim parts of the valley for their homesteads, using military land grants awarded them for fighting under Jackson.[8]

Such was the case with Jesse Wilson, a former soldier, who is reputed to be the first white man to settle in what would become Montevallo. On a hill overlooking Shoal Creek, Jesse Wilson built his cabin and planted a corn crop in 1814, very soon after the land had been forcibly ceded by the Muscogee people. Wilson's family and friends followed his lead and claimed their homesteads in this small, burgeoning community known then as Wilson's Hill.[9]

Edmund King did not serve in General Jackson's regiments, but he surely knew that fertile, cultivated land in and near the Cahaba Valley would soon be auctioned at US government land offices. King may have been encouraged to explore this region by his cousin, William Rufus King, who after serving three terms in Congress came to present-day Selma and Cahawba, Alabama, in early 1818 and with family members developed what would become one of the largest cotton plantations in Alabama, where as many as five hundred enslaved people labored.[10]

By whatever means Edmund King learned of this recently ceded land, he became one of the first elite white settlers to claim large tracts at Wilson's Hill in 1817. And then, between 1823 and 1828, he purchased at government auctions several thousand more acres of that former Muscogee land in Shelby, Bibb, and Chilton counties.[11]

After Congress passed President Andrew Jackson's Indian Removal Act in 1830, forcing Muscogee, Cherokee, Choctaw, and Chickasaw people onto trails of tears headed west, Edmund King acquired another 9,600 acres in eight Alabama counties (Shelby, Talladega, Chilton, Bibb, Pickens, Sumter, Clay, and St. Clair).[12]

Exactly what King did with those thousands of acres in other counties deserves further investigation. He may have resold the land for a handsome profit as other enslavers were migrating into the state. He may have given parcels of land to founders of new companies as a means of investment and gaining a financial stake in those companies—such as the Tuscaloosa Manufacturing Company, which launched a massive textile mill and factory in Bibb County in 1836 that produced and manufactured osnaburg, the rough-hewn fabric enslaved people were forced to wear. Twenty-one years later, in 1857, the business was offered for sale in a large advertisement in the Tuscaloosa *Independent Monitor*, placed by the then-president of the Tuscaloosa Manufacturing Company, Edmund King.[13]

Let's never forget that King's extensive and diversified investment in agriculture, ironworks, the building of railroads, mining, and companies such as the Tuscaloosa Manufacturing Company were dependent on the prior dispossession of Muscogee people, and the capital assets and privileges he acquired as an enslaver. That is why, when I speak or write about my Montevallo ancestors, I don't simply say that they were enslavers. I say that they were enslavers who accumulated great wealth through two systems of theft.

The Role White Women Played in Supporting and Perpetuating Slavery

The second realm of investigation that deserves our attention is the role white women played in supporting, defending, maintaining, and perpetuating enslavement. It has often been assumed that the worst forms of brutality during slavery were inflicted on people working in the fields, and the "great house" (aka King House) was a safer place. Closely aligned with this assumption is another: namely, that white men inflicted violence and enforced the strictures of slavery far more than white women. Both assumptions need to be critically interrogated as we examine primary sources of enslavement in Montevallo.

I am particularly indebted to the work that historians Thavolia Glymph and Stephanie Jones-Rogers have done in this regard. In *Out of the House of Bondage*, Glymph notes that far too much silence surrounds the roles that white women played in supporting, maintaining, and participating in what Glymph calls the "maiming and destruction of black life." Slave ownership conferred the abuse of power on all white people, not just on white men. Therefore, says Glymph, "The great house, whether a six-columned mansion or a rude house of four rooms, was a space of slavery and, thus, of domination and subordination."[14]

We who are gathered to speak of King House might elaborate on Glymph's statement by saying, "The great house, whether a six-columned mansion, a rude house of four rooms, or a two-story Federal-style brick house adorned with glass windows, was a space of slavery and, thus, of domination and subordination."

I want to highlight another phrase Glymph uses when describing plantation households like King House. She says they were "site[s] of struggle between women" because the domestic realm was a site of power for white women and a site of exploitation and violence for Black women.[15] White "mistresses" (as they were called) were not, of course, equal legally to the white masters, but that does not mean that white women never acted on their own authority to enforce and maintain their dominance and control.

In *They Were Her Property*, Stephanie Jones-Rogers challenges the contention of many historians that white women who were raised in slaveholding families or who married slaveholding men participated in slavery only vicariously. She contends that scholars frequently have concluded that when women exercised authority over enslaved people, these women did so reluctantly, from a sense of marital obligation rather than their authority, governance, and discipline being "voluntary or self-initiated, management and discipline of enslaved people."[16] Jones-Rogers points out that this conclusion fails to account for the significant number of white women who themselves owned slaves—by means of inheritance or by purchases they initiated.

Also overlooked are the slaveholding women whom men married to enhance their economic status and reputation. As Jones-Rogers has noted, "Simply by marrying a woman with property, even if she maintained control of it, a man could improve his position: husbands often borrowed money from their wives and used the enslaved people their wives inherited to cultivate the lands they bought with those loans."[17]

At least one of Edmund King's daughters, Elizabeth, matches exactly the social and economic position that Jones-Rogers has described: She became an owner of slaves, and her husband, George Shortridge, used the enslaved people she owned to borrow money, purchase additional property, and seek to pay his debts.

I have spent the past four years doing intensive research about Elizabeth King Shortridge because she is the person in the King family tree through whom I am directly related to Edmund King. Elizabeth King Shortridge is the grandmother of my father's grandmother—Marie Shortridge Morrison—who was born in King House in 1867.

George and Elizabeth Shortridge lived on a Montevallo plantation called Holly Brook. Golda Johnson, in *The Lives and Times of Kingswood*, tells us that George, Elizabeth, and their youngest children moved from Holly Brook into King House in 1860 to care for Elizabeth's aging father, Edmund. Before Edmund died in 1863, he willed King House to George and Elizabeth, and they lived in King House until George's death in 1870.[18]

Books written about notable men of Alabama often mention George Shortridge. Partly due to these publications, George earned a reputation as a scholar, circuit court judge, and 1855 gubernatorial candidate that lived on for generations after his death. But when it came to financial matters, Elizabeth's father, Edmund King, carried far more economic clout and prestige than her husband. Not only did George have a fraction of the enslaved people Edmund owned, he also repeatedly spent more money than he earned and lost a great deal of money on bad investments. George frequently had to mortgage the people he enslaved to get the loans he needed. That became a vicious cycle for him. When he couldn't repay the loans, he was in danger of losing the people he held in bondage.[19]

I have found considerable evidence that Edmund King harbored abiding concerns about his son-in-law's economic viability. For the sake of his daughter,

Elizabeth, King bailed George out of bankruptcy more than once.[20] Over the course of many years, Edmund gave Elizabeth several enslaved people as "gifts" and specified that she was to be the owner, not George. And shortly before his death in 1863, Edmund stipulated in a deed that $4,000 in interest on a note be held in trust for his daughter Elizabeth "for her sole and separate use and benefit free from the controle [sic] and management of her husband."[21]

In October 2022, I stood in the Shelby County Museum and Archives, straining to steady my camera above a deed recorded on August 5, 1844. My hands shook as I sought to capture the image. In that deed, Edmund King declared that "in consideration of the mutual love and affection" he held for his daughter, Elizabeth, he had chosen to give, grant, and convey to her "a certain negro girl named Amanda aged about nine years, and her future increase" (meaning her children, grandchildren, and great-grandchildren).[22]

In one brief paragraph, that document revealed so many soul-splitting assumptions held by white enslavers and concealed so many deprivations experienced by the Black women and girls whom King enslaved. In that deed, Edmund King celebrated the loving bond that he and Elizabeth shared while legally severing Amanda's familial bonds. As legal scholar Margaret Burnham notes, the laws of enslavement treated each slave "as an individual unit of property, and never as a submerged partner in a marriage or family." Love, marriage, procreation, and childrearing "were manipulated to meet the demands of the commercial enterprise."[23]

This deed proclaimed to whom Amanda belonged: Edmund King. He was entitled to do with her whatever he wished, regardless of the repercussions. Not only was she treated as an instrument of reproduction capable of birthing children, thereby increasing his financial assets, she was also his sexual property, as Margaret Burnham states: "available to be raped and sexually abused with impunity by the slaveholder, his sons, the overseer, or any other white man."[24] And he chose on August 5, 1844, to give nine-year-old Amanda to Elizabeth.

As I stood in the Shelby County Courthouse 178 years later, I trembled as I read this deed. Earlier that day my sister, Stephanie, had texted me a photo of her precious nine-year-old granddaughter, Lydia Rose, dancing on the sidewalk in front of her school.

There is another dimension of this deed that must be named, faced, and grappled with. It stipulated that nine-year-old Amanda would remain Elizabeth's possession for her entire natural life. And after Elizabeth's death, Amanda and her children were to be divided equally among Elizabeth's heirs. Let's just take a moment and let that sink in.

This entire transaction is embedded in the belief that slavery would remain in place for generations to come. There is no mention of Amanda's mother, father, and siblings or future family bonds that would be severed. According to Edmund King and the state of Alabama, Amanda and her children were to be property of Elizabeth's descendants, for generations to come.

Stephanie Jones-Rogers provides numerous testimonies by formerly enslaved people who experienced exploitation and abuse at the hands of white "mistresses." As Jones-Rogers says:

> No group spoke about [white] women's investments in slavery more often, or powerfully, than the enslaved people subjected to their ownership and control. They were the people whose lives were forever changed when a mistress sold someone just so she could buy a new dress. They were best equipped to describe the agony that shook their bodies and souls when they returned from their errands to discover that their children were gone and their mistresses were counting piles of money they had received from the slave traders who bought them. Only enslaved people could speak about their female owners' profound economic contributions to their continued enslavement with such astonishing precision.[25]

Precisely how Elizabeth King Shortridge managed, rewarded, and punished the enslaved women she owned or oversaw in Holly Brook and in King House, I do not yet know. I have not yet come upon first-person narratives from the women or men she enslaved. But I do have deeds and estate papers that witness to Elizabeth's "profound economic contributions" to the continued enslavement of nine-year-old Amanda, fourteen-year-old Minerva, twenty-seven-year-old Caroline, her two children, and "a negro girl named Sely."

When we read or hear about enslavers in Montevallo, it is almost exclusively male enslavers, like Edmund King, that are named. The role that white women played in supporting, defending, maintaining, and perpetuating enslavement must be investigated, collected, and shared in the deeper, truer King House narratives.

Stories of Audacious Resistance and Resilience

The third realm of investigation that deserves our attention is the myriad ways enslaved people resisted and subverted slavery's assault on their bodies, their minds, their souls, their families, their communities, their beliefs, and their spiritual practices.

Historian Stephanie Camp wrote a very important, and often cited, book in 2004 titled *Closer to Freedom: Enslaved Women and Everyday Resistance in the Plantation South*. Camp invites us to understand the day-to-day resistance of enslaved people in multiple ways and to refrain from equating resistance with the most visible and organized forms of opposition, namely armed rebellions. Those uprisings and insurgencies were very significant forms of resistance, but so were the everyday acts that slowed or interrupted the plantation's rigid labor system. Enslaved people sought out spaces free of white oversight where they could experience rest and revival for their bodies and spirits.[26]

Enslavers sought to build what Stephanie Camp calls a "geography of containment," in which the movement of enslaved people was confined and controlled by slave patrols, passes, curfews, shackles, threats of violence, prohibitions against community gatherings, and monitored breaks and holidays. Confinement and control were resisted by developing "a rival geography" in spaces free from white oversight and control. Camp cites testimonies from Works Progress Administration narratives and other sources that describe how enslaved people slipped away from their cabins at night to attend parties, make music, dance and socialize, in outbuildings, woods, swamps, and neighboring farms. In those spaces they engaged in creative expression, networking, worship, and community celebrations for the birth of a baby or a wedding.[27]

Some enslaved people resisted confinement and violence by seeking their freedom as fugitives. The 1860 census recorded that Edmund King owned twenty-five men, women, and children—eight of whom were marked in the census as "fugitive."[28] The instructions for the census taker stressed the importance of noting which slaves were fugitives because those slaves were still property of the enslaver—in this case Edmund King. If those eight check marks under the heading of "fugitive slave" are accurate, we must ask what would prompt five mulatto men ranging in age from eighteen to sixty; two mulatto women, ages twenty-eight and forty-five; and one thirteen-year-old mulatto girl to risk the attendant dangers of fleeing the King plantation, seeking their freedom by journeying hundreds of miles usually on foot.

Far more frequent than seeking freedom as a fugitive was the practice of truancy. "For periods lasting a night, a week, or several weeks, enslaved women and men ran away to nearby woods, swamps, and the slave quarters of neighboring plantations."[29] Truancy was often a response to a particular grievance or act of violence they had suffered. Enslaved women engaged in truancy as a way of escaping, or at least getting a break from, violations of their bodies by white men who sexually assaulted them, or by the ill-tempered white women who punished them. Enslaved women also assisted the practice of absenteeism by feeding truants or giving them shelter.[30]

Truancy did not go unpunished, and, as Camp notes, the fact "that enslaved people were willing to risk gruesome punishments for the sake of a degree of mobility speaks volumes about its importance to them."[31] Sometimes, enslavers chose not to inflict severe punishments because they needed the labor of truant individuals when they returned. And most people did return—for the sake of their children, out of hunger, and suffering from heat or cold.

When enslaved women enacted everyday resistance by taking food home to their children from the great house, slowing their pace of work, or leaving tasks unfinished, white women complained that Black women were by nature slovenly, savage, or uncivilized. The resistance of enslaved women within the white household and the subsequent complaints about their "insubordination" stand in sharp contrast to Golda Johnson's use of the term "faithful and devoted servants" when referring to the people Edmund King enslaved, and to her assertion in *The Lives and Times of Kingswood* that "many slaves were contented, if not happy. Some were as close to the master as other members of the household."

Another form of resistance by enslaved women and men was to undertake every means at their disposal to prevent the rupture of their families. Two years ago, while searching for deeds in the Shelby County Museum and Archives, I came upon a stunning example of this resistance.

A deed signed on February 6, 1855, recorded that Edmund King received $1,600 from a woman named Sukey, and $1 from George Shortridge (who was married to King's daughter, Elizabeth). Deed books are rife with transactions between Montevallo enslavers like Edmund King and George Shortridge who were buying or selling land and property, including the people they enslaved. But this deed is extraordinary because it says that $1,600 was given Edmund King not for an enslaved woman, but by a woman whom he enslaved. That woman was Sukey.[32]

You might be wondering: How in the world could an enslaved woman have earned and saved that much money? Sukey may have possessed a skill in high demand by neighboring enslavers. Perhaps she was a seamstress, renowned for designing gowns that white women wore at festive occasions like weddings. Or she may have been a midwife, hired by neighboring enslavers to care for the reproductive health of their enslaved women or to provide help at the births of their own children.[33] If Edmund King hired Sukey out to enslaver friends and neighbors, he may have permitted her to keep a portion of that rental income, which she saved over many years.

There are court records in the Shelby County Archives indicating that Edmund King contracted some of his slaves to others, thereby permitting them to earn overtime wages. For example, in June 1859, the Third District of the Shelby County Circuit Court issued an indictment of Edmund King for permitting a slave named George to "hire himself to said person, or to hire him overtime, or to go at large against the peace and dignity of the state of Alabama."[34]

When I first read the deed about Sukey giving money to Edmund King, I wondered if she was purchasing her freedom. But that was impossible because self-manumission was strictly prohibited in Alabama in 1855. Closer inspection revealed that Sukey's intent with this payment was to keep her family intact. This deed recorded that George Shortridge purchased Sukey's daughters, Margaret (twenty-two) and Ann (sixteen), from Edmund King for $1 and agreed to serve as their trustee. It also enumerated three conditions that placed strict limitations on George's ownership and protected Sukey's daughters: (1) George could not, under any circumstances, mortgage Margaret and Ann as collateral or sell them to pay his debts; (2) Margaret and Ann were to have "the privilege of living with their mother"; and (3) if George should predecease Margaret or Ann, they were to have the privilege and power "to choose and select another Trustee."[35]

Sukey's $1,600 purchased the guarantee that Margaret and Ann would not be sold away from her. That guarantee was a monumental achievement. Enslaved people lived with a constant fear of being separated from the people they loved. When enslavers like Edmund King and George Shortridge wanted to acquire more land, livestock, machinery, or slaves, they financed their purchases by using the slaves they already owned as collateral for loans. And when they could not pay creditors, relinquishing those enslaved people was the means of settling the debt. That meant that enslaved people were always at risk of being mortgaged or sold. Without warning, they could be separated from their family and community if their enslaver became overextended financially.

The restrictions on George's ownership of Margaret and Ann proved to be prescient. In 1858, George Shortridge was on the brink of insolvency. On May 4 of that year, he named nine of his enslaved people as collateral for "several debts... to various creditors."[36] If he could not honor those debts, those nine people would be given to his creditors as payment. Margaret and Ann may have overheard rumors and complaints about George's indebtedness rumbling through the Shortridge household and insisted they be returned to the King plantation—as was their right in the original deed of trust negotiated with Edmund King.

In January 1859, George Shortridge filed a quitclaim deed, stating that he transferred title to Margaret, Ann, and a young child of Margaret's back to Edmund King "at the instance and request of a Negro girl Sukey of copper color about fifty years of age and Margaret a girl of Mullato color about twenty six years of age & her increase and Anny of Mullato color about twenty years of age."[37]

Once again, it is striking to read how Sukey exercised her agency, joined this time by the agency of her daughters, Margaret and Ann (Anny).

These three deeds provide fragments of a remarkable story that occurred in the decade preceding emancipation. In an oppressive system that fostered the sexual exploitation of enslaved women and robbed them of "social standing, political power, [and] economic means," Sukey summoned extraordinary strength and courage to prevent the fracturing of her family and move three generations further down the road toward freedom.[38]

In forging deeper, truer King House narratives, it is of crucial importance that these stories of resistance and resilience be retrieved, collected, and shared.

In April 2022, when we gathered in the Carmichael Library for the day-long conference titled Why We Must Remember, I spoke of my belief that there is a deep yearning in this nation for remembering, truth telling, and reckoning with the history of enslavement and with the history of what journalist Nikole Hannah-Jones calls "the audacious resistance and resilience of Black Americans."[39] I want to reiterate that conviction today despite escalating efforts by some to restrict and censure the study and teaching of those histories.

Remembering and reckoning with the legacies of slavery can be hard, gut-wrenching, even excruciating, but I don't believe it is divisive work that results in useless guilt or self-loathing. Quite the contrary. I believe it is life-giving work for all of us. It is an invitation to love ourselves, others, and our country enough to do the deep work of truth telling and healing so that together we might repair the breaches that racism creates. It is an invitation to break the silences and rebuild the foundations of our communities.

12

Letter to My Great-Great-Great-Grandmother, Elizabeth King Shortridge

We can't alter the actions of our ancestors, but we can decide what to do with the social relations they left us.... Knowing, honestly examining, and taking full responsibility for what our ancestors left us is both a spiritual and a political practice of integrity and authenticity, empowering and radical and strategically essential. —AURORA LEVINS MORALES, "Raícism," 2019

Early in my ancestral investigations, I discovered that my great-great-great-grandmother, Elizabeth King Shortridge (1817–1905), is known as "the first white child" born in Montevallo, Alabama. Because of my direct lineage to Elizabeth (she is the grandmother of my father's grandmother), I spent time making notes about her life as the daughter of enslavers. I wanted to learn how the ideology of white supremacy, the economic and social structure of slavery, and the politics of gender and class had shaped the woman she became.

Elizabeth was eighteen when she married George D. Shortridge, also of Montevallo. George's people were enslavers who came south from Kentucky in 1822.

In my feverish search for a diary or letters written by Elizabeth, I discovered the George D. Shortridge Family Papers. Housed at the Briscoe Center for American History in Austin, Texas, this archival trove contains 122 letters, spanning seven decades from 1846 to 1902. My initial disappointment at finding no letters penned by Elizabeth was assuaged by the realization that most of the letters were written to her. In fact, this collection might have more appropriately been named the Elizabeth King Shortridge Family Papers.

Elizabeth received letters written in pencil from the battlefields where her three sons were fighting for the Confederacy. She received numerous letters of condolence from friends and family when hearing of the losses she sustained during the early 1860s, including the death of her father and the death of two sons killed in combat. While serving as circuit judge in different counties, her husband, George, often wrote Elizabeth about cases he adjudicated. In later years, grandchildren wrote Elizabeth about their jobs, their children, and their longing to see her. The content and tenor of these letters reveal that Elizabeth was a woman that friends and family loved and trusted with their aspirations, anxieties, and confessions.

It may have been Elizabeth herself who saved, gathered, and donated these letters to the Briscoe Center in the hope that they would be of significance to future researchers and descendants. Whatever her reasons for saving and bundling these letters, I am grateful that they were archived. They open a window into aspects of Elizabeth's life that would have otherwise been inaccessible to me.

I have read and reread those letters, asking what it means to be Elizabeth's descendant. I compiled a list of questions I would ask Elizabeth if only I could reach her across the ancestral eons that separate us. Sometimes I paced back and forth in my study aching to hear what Elizabeth would say in response. One morning in April 2021, I was seized by the thought of writing my letters to Elizabeth—as her great-great-great-granddaughter. The first letter poured out of me. I held nothing back. And others followed day by day.

This one-way correspondence has become an indispensable part of my ancestral investigations. Writing to Elizabeth opens new questions that I need to research, and the subsequent research inspires me to engage with Elizabeth in new ways.

When I was invited to present a keynote speech at the University of Montevallo in April 2022, I wrote Elizabeth, telling her I would be giving a talk about her Montevallo home, her family of origin, and the people they enslaved.

March 21, 2022

Dear Elizabeth,

In three weeks, I will rise before the sun, haul my suitcases to the car, and depart on a 770-mile drive to Montevallo. I've been invited to deliver a lecture at the University of Montevallo titled "Why We Must Remember: A King Descendant's Reckoning with Her Slaveholding Ancestors."

I'll be speaking to faculty and students from the university and to leaders from the surrounding community. The conference theme is why we must remember the profound impact that slavery has had on our nation. Half of this daylong conference will be focused on King House.

This will be the first time I have publicly acknowledged being a direct descendant of ancestors who for generations accumulated wealth on the backs of enslaved Africans. In the forty minutes allotted me, I will be revealing things I have learned about you, Elizabeth, and others in your extended family. I'm going to tell the story of visiting the King family cemetery and learning that there is no comparable cemetery where Black descendants can pay their respects at the graves of their ancestors. I will probably cite passages from your husband's incendiary defense of white supremacy in his 1859 *De Bow's* essay. I'll share how nothing could have prepared me for seeing the names of the men, women, and children your father bought and sold as property. I may describe how Black people whom you and George enslaved lived in constant fear of being sold to pay off George's debts. I may also share something of Sukey's story. How she may have labored for years to purchase trusteeship guarantees from your father and negotiate a way to keep her family intact.

I wonder how you will feel about my speaking publicly and naming things I have learned about the King and Shortridge families, the two families you brought together when you married George.

It is possible that some people present at my lecture, or hearing later about it, may rise to your defense, accusing me of painting an unnecessarily critical portrait, insisting that the Kings and Shortridges were highly respected families who provided exemplary leadership and spurred needed commercial development in Montevallo's early years.

I doubt there will be people in attendance who will seek to defend the institution of slavery itself, but some may argue that it is unfair to impose a modern worldview on people who were raised in a very different time. Others may insist that little can be gained from dwelling on slavery that everyone now agrees was wrong. We should focus instead on what we hold in common as Americans and move forward.

Elizabeth, for years, I have longed to discover a female ancestor in the branches of my family tree whom I can call upon for strength and guidance on days like this—as I head south to give this lecture, unsure who will be in that audience. I've spent countless hours reading the biographies and narratives of white abolitionists, praying a document would suddenly appear as evidence that someone in my family tree resisted or interrupted racism. By writing a letter to the editor. By attending an abolitionist gathering. By signing an antilynching petition. By preaching a sermon that condemns segregation. By spending a night in jail after being arrested at a sit-in.

I can proudly call the names of my parents, Truman Aldrich Morrison Jr. and Eleanor Shelton Morrison, grateful for all they modeled for me by speaking up and speaking out against racist policies where they lived, worked, and worshipped. But I haven't yet found one shred of evidence that points to an antiracist ancestor in previous generations.

After years of longing and searching for antiracist ancestors, I feel as though I am being led down another path that offers me a different kind of spiritual grounding and sustenance. That path has brought me to you, Elizabeth. It has also led me to work with people currently living in Montevallo who are passionate about addressing the egregious harm caused by the forced removal of the Muscogee people and by the enslavement of African Americans. I am keenly aware that you and your parents benefited mightily from both of those systems of theft.

There is so much work to be done if amends are to be made and the legacies of slavery are to be remedied. Telling the truth about King House, the brutality of enslavement, and its enduring legacies is but one step on the road to reparations. But even those acts of repair are being strenuously opposed in high places. As of January 2022, twenty-nine states had introduced bills limiting how public school teachers can talk about racism, restricting a fuller and more truthful study of slavery. Just four days ago, Alabama's House of Representatives, by a vote of 65–32, passed a bill that will restrict what teachers can say about systemic racism and the history of slavery.

I don't want to turn from you, Elizabeth. I want to turn toward you. I want to know who you were so I can better understand how I have been shaped by the legacies of my ancestors. And I want you to know who I am and why I keep returning to Montevallo.

When I address the gathering in Montevallo on April 14, I will be testifying to the responsibility I bear as your descendant.

                                  Your great-great-great-granddaughter,
                                  Melanie
                                  Okemos, Michigan

III. LEGACIES OF LYNCHING

13

Soul Splitting

The trauma of racism is, for the racist and the victim, the severe fragmentation of the self.—TONI MORRISON, "Unspeakable Things Unspoken," 2018

For years, I have been haunted by the image of my grandfather as a young child standing with his father in the midst of a lynch mob. He is seven or eight years old, holding his breath and squeezing his daddy's hand tighter and tighter as screams pierce the humid Alabama night air.

The origin of this image is not derived from a family story, photograph, or any factual evidence. The fearful thought that my grandfather might have witnessed a lynching first occurred to me in the summer of 2006 as I stood, scarcely breathing, in front of a life-size photograph of a lynching displayed in the National Civil Rights Museum in Memphis, Tennessee. The crowd of white people was so large that the photograph covered an entire wall. I had rounded a corner at the museum and was suddenly face-to-face with white men, women, and children—many smiling at the photographer, none hiding their faces in shame while the desecrated body of a Black man hung from a nearby tree.

I had previously beheld horrifying photographs of lynchings in books or magazines. But not before I stood at that wall, my legs shaking and my heart pounding, had I ever entertained the thought that some of my ancestors could have participated in a lynching.

Two years later, during one of my weekly visits with Aunt Harriet, I asked whether she had ever heard talk about her father being taken to a lynching as a child. Clearly affronted by the question, she insisted that she had never heard such a thing and then declared, "Besides, if my father had ever witnessed such a terrible thing, he would never have talked about it!"

Because I know so little about my great-grandfather, I do not know if he would have taken his sons to lynchings as a ritualistic rite of passage into white manhood. What I do know is this: By the time my grandfather was fifteen years old, ten Black men had been lynched within a fifteen-mile radius of the two Alabama towns in which he lived—Blocton and Ensley.

Ten human beings wrenched from their families—hunted down, abducted, and brutalized. Ten Black men, survived by spouses and children, mothers and fathers, sisters and brothers. Ten acts of terrorism inflicted on an entire Black community in those towns. Ten horrific murders that left Black families and communities physically and emotionally scarred for generations.

These were the ten lynchings reported in Alabama newspapers between 1893 and 1909. The actual number of victims is likely greater. In that same time period, 175 Black men statewide were lynched and hundreds more in neighboring states.

Whether or not my grandfather was physically present, the phenomenon of lynching was stitched into the fabric of everyday life in his Alabama childhood and adolescence. In 1892, the year before my grandfather's birth, more than 250 Black people were lynched throughout the United States—the highest number recorded for any single year.[1] White newspapers in the towns where he was raised frequently reported lynchings that occurred throughout the state and the region, often replete with graphic details of how the victim died. As Jacqueline Goldsby notes, "Spread across a front page or crowding an inside page with a series of long columns, these reports were impossible to ignore. Though the journalistic coverage ostensibly was meant to inform the public about the incident, these accounts actually compounded the violence by turning readers into both voyeurs and victims."[2]

Undoubtedly, my grandfather heard about lynchings as his father or mother read aloud the latest newspaper account. Surely, he knew classmates who bragged that their family members had witnessed a lynching. Friends may have relished telling him tall tales about what they saw or did at the lynching. He was certain to overhear adults talking in public places about the precipitating offense, the impressive size of the crowd, or the fruitless pleading of the victim. Perhaps some childhood friend invited my grandfather to his home after school and proudly showed him a photograph from the crime scene or produced a relic that the family was saving to commemorate the atrocity: a block of charred wood, a piece of rope, the remnant of clothing, or a body part.

Lynching was a systematic form of torture and terror perpetrated by white people for decades in this country. It is an indisputable fact that many of us who are white have ancestors who personally witnessed and perhaps even instigated lynchings. Yet I had seldom had a conversation with another white person about this aspect of our family histories. Not until I undertook this research. In my experience, the silence in white families and white communities about lynching is almost complete.

Nearly fifty years after the lynching of Matthew Williams in Salisbury and George Armwood in Princess Anne, University of Maryland Law School professor Sherrilyn Ifill undertook intensive investigations of these acts of terror perpetrated on the Eastern Shore of Maryland in the early 1930s. As she interviewed Black and white residents of Salisbury and Princess Anne, Ifill encountered a recurring pattern. Black residents recalled in vivid detail the events surrounding the lynchings. Many could identify a family member who heard the horrific sounds emanating from the site of the lynching or saw the victim's body the next day. By contrast, the white residents of Salisbury and Princess Anne consistently denied any knowledge of the lynching and "almost to a person, nearly every white person insisted that the lynchers were from 'out of town.'"[3]

The facts contradict the testimonies of these white residents. When Matthew Williams was dragged from his hospital bed and lynched on the courthouse lawn in 1931, Salisbury, Maryland, had nine thousand white residents. By all accounts, as many as one thousand white people may have witnessed some part of the lynching that night. As Ifill notes, "this means that perhaps 10 percent of the town's white population saw the lynching. Yet sixty-eight years later, when I talked with residents, very few whites admitted that they or their families had any personal recollection of the lynching. And so this event, which had constituted a defining racial moment in the Black community, had virtually no contemporary significance for whites."[4]

Furthermore, being physically present or actively participating in the crime was not the only measure of complicity. Lynchings were not isolated and random events shrouded in secrecy. Word of the impending violence spread through white communities and—in the aftermath—photographs, postcards, relics, and newspaper reports purposely guaranteed that every member of the community would be given the opportunity to be a spectator. Nevertheless, rarely did white people intervene to help quell the escalating frenzy or demand that perpetrators of the lynching be brought to justice.

The Black people Ifill interviewed in Salisbury and Princess Anne were not focused on the instigators of the violence. Their memories were fixed on the thousands of white people who watched, stood by, or later learned about the lynching and did nothing: "For many blacks on the Shore, this was the lesson of lynching passed down from generation to generation: ordinary whites were not to be trusted."[5]

I do not know whether my grandfather was taken to a lynching, but I cannot erase the image of an eight-year-old white boy holding his daddy's hand on a hot Alabama night while unspeakable violence was perpetrated by his people.

What did he feel? Did he close his eyes or stand transfixed? Was he mute, or did he add his cracking voice to the roaring crowd as it hurled epithets at the brutalized body that swayed lifelessly from the tree limb? What did this eight-year-old child make of the cold shiver of fear that shot through his veins? Did he look up at his daddy's face, hoping to see a glimmer of his horror mirrored there? Where did he seek comfort if his father was smiling down at him, nodding with satisfaction that justice had been done?

What kind of soul splitting occurred in that child on that hot Alabama night? What manner of spiritual, emotional numbing took root in him? Where did his soul find refuge or retreat? Did it split off forever from his white body? What did he use to fill the void when it left? How did that experience shape the man he became and the father he was to his son?

I met my grandfather twice. Once when I was thirteen, on a family trip to Birmingham. Then, ten years later, when my brother and I flew to Birmingham so we could together say goodbye to him as he was dying of colon cancer. I barely knew Truman Aldrich Morrison Sr. and would be hard pressed to describe his physical features save for the photographs in our family albums. What I know of him comes through my father's stories, as well as the grief and shame that sometimes overtook my father when speaking of his father's alcoholism and physical abuse. Yet there are few people who have more profoundly shaped my life.

Because my father could not or would not undertake the healing work he needed to do, my grandfather's disappointment and rage continued to haunt his days and keep him up at night. The anxiety my grandfather instilled was channeled through my father and came to rest on my young shoulders. It took years of searching and remembering in the presence of therapists before I could name the source of this weight, recognize that it was not mine to carry, and find the inner freedom to lay it down.

As I engage in a different kind of searching and remembering now, asking how white supremacy has infected, distorted, and weakened the spiritual and emotional lives of white people, I wonder why so little attention has been given to naming and describing the intergenerational legacies of white supremacy. We can go to any bookstore and find whole sections devoted to the intergenerational legacies left by physical abuse and alcohol. I have searched in vain, however, for even one ethnographic study of white children who were present at lynchings.

Some attention has been given to the impact on white children by scholars who have studied the photographs and postcards taken as souvenirs at lynchings. James Allen, author of *Without Sanctuary*, suggests that lynching was a form of indoctrination for white children, the place where they were taught to look but not see. Learning to look and not apprehend what they were seeing became a means of "domesticating terror, normalizing it, and producing a numbing effect that allowed its perpetuation."[6]

In her essay "Lynching Photographs and the Politics of Public Shaming," art historian Dora Apel agrees that lynchings served to domesticate terror, but she believes the numbing effect was not transmitted primarily through these episodic eruptions of racialized violence. Looking at Black people but not seeing their humanity was a habitual practice for Southern white children, and it was taught in myriad forms of social interaction. "Such children not only witnessed the subordination of blacks to whites in public and private life, but also perpetuated that subordination daily, in ways inappropriate to their age and station. The lynching scene was an extreme culmination of daily practice and made possible the acceptance of lynching itself."[7]

The soul splitting that I imagine as I picture that eight-year-old white boy holding his daddy's hand did not begin or end at the lynching. It was instilled as a daily dose of white supremacist indoctrination by parents, teachers, preachers, and other significant adults.

Whether it was the primary site of indoctrination or the extreme culmination of a hundred daily habits, the silence about lynchings and what our white ancestors witnessed and perpetrated must be broken. A naming and accountability must begin. As Ifill says, "It is in the telling *and hearing* of formerly silenced stories that communities can re-create themselves."[8] If our genealogical investigations fail to enumerate the enormous costs that lynching exacted, we will be guilty of fabricating an invented past.

14

Researching Injustice

TELLING THE STORY OF LEGAL LYNCHING
IN JIM CROW BIRMINGHAM

After the publication of Murder on Shades Mountain: The Legal Lynching of Willie Peterson and the Struggle for Justice in Jim Crow Birmingham *in March 2018, I went on a seventeen-city tour. This lecture was delivered on June 7, 2018, at the Arcus Center for Social Justice Leadership in Kalamazoo, Michigan.*

On August 4, 1931, three white women were brutally attacked on Shades Mountain at the southeastern edge of Birmingham, Alabama. The sole survivor, Nell Williams, who was eighteen years old, said they had taken a ride up the mountain in the late afternoon to sit on some boulders and look out on the valley below. She told authorities that just as they returned to their car, "a Negro wielding a gun" jumped on the running board of their car and held the women captive for four hours—lecturing them about the evils of the white race before shooting them and disappearing into the woods. Nell's sister, Augusta Williams, was mortally wounded that night, and their friend, Jennie Wood, died nine days later in a Birmingham hospital.

Later that night, the Jefferson County Sheriff's Department and the Birmingham police deputized 250 white men for what became the largest manhunt in Jefferson County history. A reign of terror was unleashed on Birmingham's Black community. It is not hyperbolic to say that every Black man leaving Birmingham by train, by bus, by car, or on foot was suspect. Within the coming days and weeks, dozens of Black men were arrested and detained in towns and cities throughout the South and as far away as Chicago. Several Black men were killed by white vigilantes, posing as police. Rumors of communist conspiracy raged through white Birmingham for weeks as Nell Williams was unable to positively identify any of the suspects brought to her.

I want to remind us of some historical context before continuing with this story. By August 1931, just two years after the stock market crash, the steel mills had all but ceased to operate in Birmingham. Unemployed workers struggled to stave off homelessness and hunger, and hardest hit of all was Birmingham's Black community. Also, just five months before the murders on Shades Mountain, nine young Black men who came to be known as the "Scottsboro Boys" were falsely accused of raping two white women on a train traveling through rural Alabama about one hundred miles northeast of Birmingham. The Communist Party hired the lawyers who appealed the convictions of these young men and launched highly publicized international campaigns to free the defendants that shone a bright light on Jim Crow racism.

Anticommunist hysteria had reached a fever pitch in Birmingham before the attack on Shades Mountain. The manhunt for the Shades Mountain assailant became the pretext for intensifying efforts to arrest anyone suspected of being a communist sympathizer, including many in Birmingham's Black community that the white elite viewed as troublemakers.

As the manhunt stretched on and dozens of Black men were arrested, detained, and brought before Nell Williams for examination, rumors began to circulate that the women may have gone to Shades Mountain for reasons other than Nell stated. Six weeks after the attack on Shades Mountain, Nell Williams, her mother, and a family friend named Buck Strait were driving to the cemetery to put fresh flowers on Augusta Williams's grave, when Nell suddenly exclaimed, "That's the man," pointing to a Black man who was walking on a nearby sidewalk.

Buck Strait called the man to the car, pulled a pistol from the glove compartment, and held him at gunpoint until authorities arrived. Willie Peterson was the name of this man arrested at the corner of Fourteenth St. and Avenue G on a blazing hot afternoon in late September. With the exception of being Black, Willie Peterson bore little resemblance to the description Nell had originally given police. He was an unemployed miner disabled by tuberculosis. Weighing only 125 pounds at the time of his arrest, having no criminal record, and most days unable to be up and around for more than a few hours at a time, it is highly improbable that Willie Peterson would have had the physical capacity to commit the crimes that Nell Williams described. Nevertheless, Peterson was taken into custody and later indicted for murder.

The night of the arrest, 1,500 white people surrounded the Jefferson County Jail in downtown Birmingham. Fearing a lynching, Sheriff Hawkins took the prisoner out a side door and escorted him to Kilby Prison in Montgomery for safekeeping. Two weeks later, again under cover of night, Willie Peterson was returned to the Jefferson County Jail for an interrogation by fifteen white people that included two prosecuting attorneys, the chief of police, the sheriff, several officers, Nell Williams, her older brother Dent (who was a lawyer), and Nell's father and mother. Willie Peterson had no attorney, no one present to represent or support him. During that hour-long interrogation, Willie Peterson said repeatedly what he had said since the time of his arrest: "I did not kill those girls. You have the wrong Negro."

To describe what happens next, I read to you from chapter 6:

> After a full hour of questioning, Chief Fred McDuff sensed the group had grown restless and weary. He was just about to announce that they would bring things to a close when gunshots rang out.
>
> "Lord, have mercy," Willie moaned, folding his arms across his chest.
>
> Dent Williams, standing six feet from the bed, had fired five shots. Three entered Peterson's body—two in the chest and one in his arm. In the chaos that ensued, Chief McDuff grabbed Dent, who willingly surrendered the gun, saying, "I'm not going to do any more. I'm through."
>
> Peterson slumped over on the cot and said softly, "White folks, you are killing an innocent Negro."
>
> No one rushed to stanch the flow of blood, but Deputy Hollums did respond to Dent's request that "somebody catch Mother." When Hollums moved to support Mrs. Williams, thinking she might faint, she said, "I am all right."
>
> Convinced that Peterson was about to expire, Assistant Solicitor Long decided to increase the intensity of his interrogation. Hoping to use the fear of God and imminent heaven as a means of coercing a confession, Long leaned over Peterson, who was now lying on his side. "You are dying, Willie. You can't die with a lie on your lips," Long bellowed. "I am awfully sorry this has happened, but you deserve to die. You murdered two women."
>
> "No, sir, I didn't," Peterson protested. "I want to talk with my wife."

Saying there was not time to fetch her, Long promised he would personally deliver Peterson's message to his wife.

"Tell her to meet me in heaven," Peterson whispered.

Feigning misapprehension, Long reiterated the request: "Tell her you wronged her? Tell her you killed those white women?"

"No sir," Peterson said. The bloodstains on Peterson's shirt grew more visible. He drew his legs up in a fetal position to lessen the pain.... Long asked Peterson if he wanted to see his preacher....

Peterson exclaimed, "Yes, sir, get my preacher, Rev. Matthews."

Reiterating that Peterson would be dead before the preacher could get there, Long asked what message he should give Rev. Matthews.

"Tell him to keep on preaching the word," said Peterson.

"What word?" Long asked.

"The word of God."

Pretending not to hear, Long continued, "Tell him to keep preaching that Negroes are better than white folks?"

"No, sir, no, sir, that is wrong." Peterson was lying on his side, doubled up, holding his stomach.

Clark Williams interrupted, reaching over the table and motioning to Willie: "Look at me, boy, look at me. One of these women you killed told you she had a father and he was a good man."

"Captain," Peterson said, looking up at Williams, "I haven't killed anybody."

"I am the girl's father and I am a good man," said Williams. "I tell you, you can't afford to die without telling the truth. You did kill my daughter, didn't you?"

"No, sir, I didn't kill her," Peterson uttered one last time before the ambulance arrived.

As Peterson was taken out on a stretcher, Nell Williams approached Assistant Solicitor Long, saying she knew that "the Negro" would never confess before dying.

"I would know him in sixteen hundred people," she declared. "He lied."

Dent was right behind Nell, asking if he could get a bond. His father joined in, insisting he did not want his boy to spend the night in jail.

"Can't we fix a bond for him?" Clark Williams asked.

"You might, Clark," Long replied. "I have no charge against him."

Dent Williams went home to sleep in his own bed that night. Willie Peterson was taken, bleeding profusely, to Hillman Hospital, where he was not expected to live.

WILLIE PETERSON HOVERED BETWEEN life and death for several weeks, miraculously survived, and stood trial in December 1931. The local branch of the NAACP and the Communist Party vied for leadership in the case—both offering to hire and pay the legal fees of defense attorneys. The NAACP was able to convince Willie Peterson's wife, Henrietta, that she might seal her husband's fate if she hired a communist-backed attorney. Despite threats of violence by white vigilantes, Peterson's coworkers from the mines and fellow church members testified to his character, and neighbors testified they had seen Peterson on the afternoon of August 4, and he was nowhere near Shades Mountain.

After forty-four hours of deliberation, the jury reported that they were "hopelessly deadlocked," and a mistrial was declared. This stunning news swept the nation. For a jury to be "hopelessly deadlocked," at least one member of this all-white male jury had to break with a cardinal tenet of Jim Crow white supremacy: namely, if a white woman testified that a Black man committed the crime, white men were obligated to take her at her word. The Black press all across the country interpreted a hung jury as an incontestable declaration of innocence. The *Atlanta World* declared, "History was written today at the Jefferson county courthouse."

Willie Peterson's second trial was rife with judicial bias and misconduct. With one or two exceptions, the judge overruled every objection entered by defense attorneys and sustained every objection made by prosecutors. For example, during opening remarks Assistant Solicitor Long referred to the defendant as a "gorilla in human form," and the court overruled defense objections. In his instructions to the jury, the judge said, "You, as sensible men and as courageous men, must do your duty. If you fail to render a verdict in this case, you will not do your duty." This time—after only thirty minutes of deliberation—the jury found Willie Peterson guilty of murder and sentenced him to die in the electric chair.

After Willie Peterson's death sentence, the Birmingham branch of the NAACP was able to persuade the national NAACP to step up its involvement in challenging Willie Peterson's conviction and appealing his case to the Alabama Supreme Court and ultimately to the US Supreme Court. Charles Hamilton Houston became intimately involved in the case. Houston was the chief litigator for the national NAACP, dean of Howard University's Law School, and mentor to a whole generation of young Black lawyers including Thurgood Marshall.

Coming on the heels of the Scottsboro trials, the Peterson case proved to be another striking example of how courtroom trials in Jim Crow Alabama could function like lynch mobs when the defendant was Black. The notoriety of both cases gave credence to the term "legal lynching," first coined by the Communist Party in the 1920s when extrajudicial lynchings were on the decline, and the state was turning to capital punishment as the new lynching tree. During the 1930s, Alabama executed sixty-one men; all but seven were African American. Charles Hamilton Houston saw very little difference between extrajudicial lynchings carried out by white mobs and the blatant injustice meted out in Alabama courts. He believed both were forms of racial terror.

The appeal process took two years. The Alabama State Supreme Court ruled unanimously that it found nothing irregular in the second trial. When the US Supreme Court refused to hear the appeal, NAACP lawyers took the case to the governor, imploring him to grant clemency.

In March 1934, Governor Miller commuted Willie Peterson's death sentence to life in prison because of "grave doubts as to his guilt." The governor's commutation was once again front-page news in Birmingham. Commutation for a Black man convicted of killing a white woman was a rare event in Jim Crow Alabama. Governor Miller commuted the death sentence, but Willie Peterson was not released from prison. He died of tuberculosis in Kilby Prison on June 30, 1940.

I FIRST HEARD OF THIS CASE from my father, who was born and raised in Birmingham. He often told the story of the arrest and trials of Willie Peterson as a way of illustrating the injustice and violence that Black people experienced in Jim Crow Birmingham. He also told this story because it proved to be a momentous turning point in his young life. Growing up in the elite Mountain Brook section of Birmingham, the only son of a wealthy entrepreneur, my father was being groomed to take over the family business from his father, who owned gas stations and tire companies all across the city.

My father, Truman Aldrich Morrison Jr., was only thirteen years old when the murders on Shades Mountain occurred, and the events surrounding this case might not have become a momentous turning point if two other circumstances in his life had not converged. First was the fact that my father's pastor and mentor, the Rev. Henry Edmonds, was one of the influential white citizens of Birmingham who expressed doubts about Peterson's guilt and supported the NAACP appeals. The way my father told the Shades Mountain story, Henry Edmonds was the leader who spearheaded the campaign to free Willie Peterson.

The second, and equally important, circumstance in my father's life was this: When he was sixteen, my father fell in love with Genevieve Williams, the younger sister of Nell, Dent, and Augusta Williams. Torn by conflicting loyalties to his girlfriend (whom he adored) and his mentor and pastor, Henry Edmonds (whose integrity he deeply admired), my father's parochial white world began to come apart. He became obsessed with the possibility that Willie Peterson was innocent. Much to everyone's surprise, he broke off the relationship with Genevieve. He began to read books by Black writers and poets like W. E. B. Du Bois and Langston Hughes, and as a student at Birmingham-Southern College in the late 1930s he became involved in organizations that supported social equality between the races and opposed racial segregation, including the Fellowship of Reconciliation and the League of Young Southerners.

For many years, I retold the Willie Peterson story just as it was handed down to me. It was one way of accounting for the legacy of antiracist activism I inherited from my father. I have always known that my passion for racial justice and my work as an antiracism educator were seeded by the stories my father told and the lifelong activism he modeled for me. He became a pastor, but the work of dismantling racism was his deepest calling.

Two years after my father's death in 2006, I stumbled upon an article about the Shades Mountain murders that corroborated many things my father had told me. Wondering what else might have been written about this case, I launched an online search for other books and articles. In the sources I discovered, I was surprised that none featured the role Henry Edmonds played in the Peterson case. I knew my father's adoration of his mentor might have given way to hyperbole in his telling of the story, but why was there no mention of Edmonds whatsoever in these sources?

More significant still, these sources described a reign of terror carried out by law enforcement and white vigilantes in the aftermath of the murders on Shades Mountain. My father never mentioned those harrowing events. He had not told me that white vigilantes burned Black-owned businesses to the ground and pulled Black men from their beds in the middle of the night and shot them. My father did not tell us that the national NAACP and the Communist Party launched campaigns in defense of Willie Peterson. Nor did he mention that Willie Peterson's neighbors stepped forward to testify on his behalf despite threats that their homes would be burned to the ground.

I doubt that my father forgot those parts of the story or chose to keep them from me. I suspect he never knew those things as a teenager living in his insular white enclave of Mountain Brook. As I read these accounts, I realized there was a disturbing paradox at the heart of my father's story. He intended it to be an indictment of white supremacy, and yet white supremacy was replicated in and through the story that my father told and that I had repeated.

With the exception of Willie Peterson, all the people in my father's story were white. Because, as a teenager, he knew only a sliver of the larger, far more complex history of the Willie Peterson case, his story mistakenly portrayed his white pastor, Henry Edmonds, as the moral compass of the case, and it rendered invisible the Black-led organizations, as well as the friends and neighbors of Willie Peterson, that tirelessly fought for his freedom. As I reflected on this paradox, I also remembered that I was intensely interested in hearing about the Shades Mountain story from my father when I was thirteen years old because that's the year I read *To Kill a Mockingbird*—another story of Jim Crow injustice in Alabama in the early 1930s that rendered a white man, Atticus Finch, the moral hero and buried the activism and resistance of Black-led freedom movements in the 1930s.

Discovering these gaping holes in my father's story, I became intensely curious about what else I might unearth were I to undertake a serious and sustained study of this case. In November 2010, I made my first field trip to Birmingham, compelled to learn more about this case—driven as much by what my father did not tell me as by what he did.

During those first visits to Birmingham, spending time in the Birmingham Public Library Archives and seeking out people who might know about this case, two things dawned on me with great force. First, I felt even more compelled to research and write about this case, not because the injustice Willie Peterson faced was exceptional in Jim Crow Birmingham, but precisely because it was all too commonplace and because I believed that this case has much to teach us about the legacies of Jim Crow racism that continue to distort white imaginations and fuel racial disparities in arrests and sentencing today.

Second, I wished that I had begun this journey twenty years earlier. Almost eighty years had passed since the attack on Shades Mountain, and it was no longer possible to find and interview people who were old enough in 1931 to remember that event or its significance. I sought out people in Birmingham's Black community one generation removed who might have heard from their elders about the murders on Shades Mountain or the arrest of Willie Peterson. None recalled the Peterson case, but several informed me that such gross miscarriages of justice were all too common in Jim Crow Birmingham. As one man put it, "I'm surprised to learn Willie Peterson wasn't lynched by a white mob during his first night in jail."

On numerous trips to Birmingham and other cities that housed archival materials, I sought to recover every newspaper article, editorial, letter, trial transcript, city directory, sermon, photograph, census record, map, and manuscript collection of the organizations related to this case. From the start, I resolved to write a historical narrative that would be true to historical sources and accessible to a wide range of readers.

I soon discovered that existing source material provided far more documentation about the white women attacked on Shades Mountain than about the Black man accused of being their assailant. The reasons for this imbalance are manifold, with race and class being two decisive factors. Nell Williams, Augusta Williams, and Jennie Wood were daughters of affluent white families that possessed the resources to send all three to college. Willie Peterson, born into a sharecropping family in rural Alabama, worked as a child in the cotton fields and never learned to read or write. After moving to Birmingham in 1919, Peterson worked in the mines for subsistence and nonunionized wages and struggled, like most Black miners, to make ends meet.

Significant events in the lives of the Williams sisters and Jennie Wood—such as an engagement to be married—were noted in Birmingham newspapers. By contrast, Willie Peterson's name did not appear in newspapers, white or Black, until he was arrested for the Shades Mountain murders. Even then, no journalist spoke with Peterson or his family members directly, as they did with Nell Williams and her family members.

The relative dearth of information about Willie Peterson proved to be a daunting and agonizing challenge as I sought to write about him and his wife, Henrietta, with as much detail and complexity as I wrote about Nell Williams and her family. I considered interviewing the descendants of the key subjects in this case to supplement the written sources. When I discovered that Willie Peterson had no descendants, I decided to abandon that avenue of investigation, fearing that I would replicate another form of imbalance in my sources.

In my search to document this case, I spent countless hours in six different archives in different parts of the country, not resting until I was able to render Willie Peterson the subject he deserved to be in this story, not simply the object of white supremacist injustice.

The time spent in those archives was extremely valuable and enlightening, but I also needed to get out of archives and into the places where Willie Peterson had lived, worked, and worshipped. I wanted to see something of what he had seen as he moved through his world.

So, I went to the intersection of Fourteenth St. and Avenue G, where Willie Peterson was arrested, but the University of Alabama at Birmingham had completely displaced that Black neighborhood in the 1960s.

I hoped to get a glimpse of church records from the 1930s when Willie Peterson was a deacon, but the secretary at New Morning Star Baptist Church informed me that they didn't have records that went back that far.

With three friends, I went in search of Willie Peterson's neighborhood. We were unable to find the house where he and Henrietta lived at the time of his arrest. There was only a small vacant lot at that address.

I met with the owner of the Birmingham funeral home that prepared Willie Peterson's body for interment. The owner felt certain his grandfather was likely in charge of Willie's burial and was more than willing to search for records of the funeral—but was unable to recover written documents about that day.

With my spouse, April, I searched for hours for Willie Peterson's gravestone. The Birmingham Public Library archives showed the plot number and location on a map of Shadow Lawn cemetery, but many of the gravestones had been disturbed, and it may very well be that his grave never had a marker.

Even though I could not locate what I hoped to find on most of those expeditions, it was essential that I stood at the corner of Fourteenth and Avenue G; that I went to New Morning Star Baptist Church and stood at the vacant lot where Willie and Henrietta's home had been located; that I met the grandson of the funeral home director who prepared Willie Peterson's body for burial, and stood silently near his gravesite.

After my first visits to Birmingham, spending time in the Birmingham Public Library Archives and seeking out people who might know about this case, I wrote an overview of the Shades Mountain story and what I hoped to accomplish by researching and writing about this story. I shared that overview at a writing retreat I attended. When I finished, a white woman said, "That is very well written, but I am left wondering: Does the world really need another sad story?"

I was initially at a loss for words, and I returned to my room and wrote for hours—the words just pouring forth as I responded to her question: Yes, the world needs what you are calling "sad" stories as a counterweight to the preponderance of stories that have promoted social forgetting and historical amnesia. Yes, our hometowns and our schools need the truth to be told about the history of racial violence if our communities are going to become places where every child can flourish—not just some.

Yes, I wrote, the legal lynching of Willie Peterson was an excruciating story to research and write, and it is a very difficult story to read—but it is not only a sad story. It is also a story about people in Birmingham's Black community working against enormous odds to keep hope alive by their refusal to submit to the white supremacist verdict.

When the struggle for justice in Jim Crow Birmingham is commemorated today, it is events and images from the 1950s and 1960s that are most often remembered, but the 1930s in Birmingham, Alabama, were a time of intense ferment and organizing in Black communities. The more I learned about the groundbreaking work of people like Charles Hamilton Houston working in collaboration with local leaders such as Dr. Charles A. G. McPherson, secretary of the Birmingham branch of the NAACP, I knew that I was encountering the courageous predecessors of the Rev. Fred Shuttlesworth and Dr. Martin Luther King Jr. and of present-day leaders in movements such as Black Lives Matter that demand an end to racial profiling, police brutality, and the criminalization of Black men.

The struggle for justice in Jim Crow Birmingham was sustained and undergirded by countless others who kept hope alive by defying white supremacy in daily acts of courageous resistance and insubordination—like the community of family and friends who stood with Willie Peterson, remaining steadfast in their love and support right to the end. Neighbors who dared to testify at Willie's trial, supporting his alibi, despite the bands of white men who roamed the streets of Woodlawn and threatened to burn their houses to the ground. Miners, friends, and church members who sat on the witness stand at both trials attesting to Willie's integrity and honesty, and enduring insults and indignities hurled at them by prosecution lawyers. Members of New Morning Star Baptist Church who risked becoming targets of violence by signing petitions demanding that Governor Miller pardon Willie Peterson. Men and women who helped pay Willie Peterson's legal fees despite massive unemployment in the Black community during the Depression.

And Willie Peterson? Yes, he was a target of brutal injustice, but we would do him further injustice if we failed to see the steadfast faith he displayed. From the day he was arrested until the day he died, Willie Peterson maintained his innocence and never ceased believing he was worth the justice and freedom so grievously denied him. Jim Crow racism had the structural power to strip Willie Peterson of life, liberty, and the pursuit of happiness, but it could not break his spirit or coerce him into confession.

There are so many questions I would ask my father now were he still alive. I have also longed to share with him every new discovery I made about the case and how I was changed by what I learned. That's why I decided to write a letter to my father as an afterword in my book. I'd like to end with reading the last part of that letter:

> Researching and writing this book, Dad, has taught me that we who are white must always critically interrogate the stories we have inherited from our forebears, even those that have inspired our passion for justice. Because white Americans remain largely ignorant about the manifold organizations, movements, and uprisings—led by people of color—that

resisted racism in every region and every era of this country's history. Because *To Kill a Mockingbird* is still being taught as a core text about racism in three-quarters of America's public schools. Because the white savior myth not only masks the rich history of resistance and reform, it diverts attention from the real work white people need to do in collaboration with people of color.

So much work remains to be done. The demonization and criminalization of Black men remains a national disgrace. Eighty-five years after Willie Peterson was arrested on a Birmingham street corner, innocent Black men throughout the nation continue to be racially profiled, stopped and frisked, thrown to the ground, choked, shot, torn from their families, locked behind bars, and sentenced to die. Eighty-five years after the legal lynching of Willie Peterson, the death penalty is still far more likely to be sought by prosecutors and imposed by juries if the defendant is Black and the victim is white.

So much work remains to be done.

Dad, I have always admired your capacity to engage in radical self-scrutiny. It is in that spirit that I have written this letter to you. I long for the humility and courage you displayed when it came to acknowledging what you had failed to see or understand. I hope that I might be as eager to learn from those who critically interrogate the stories I tell.

With fierce hope, gratitude, and love,
Melanie

15

Trayvon Martin, the Legacy of Lynching, and the Role of White Women

Some problems we share as women, some we do not. You [white women] fear your children will grow up to join the patriarchy and testify against you; we [Black women] fear our children will be dragged from a car and shot down in the street, and you will turn your backs upon the reasons they are dying.—AUDRE LORDE, "Age, Race, Class, and Sex," 1984

I had returned to the Lillian E. Smith Center for the Arts in the mountains of north Georgia for three weeks of solitude in July 2013. I hoped to make significant headway on my research and writing about the intergenerational legacy of lynching and how this reign of terror remains largely unacknowledged by the descendants of its white perpetrators. I returned to the Lillian Smith Center not only because it offered a beautiful, secluded place to write; I wanted to do this work in a place inhabited by Lillian Smith's fierce, tenacious spirit. She has been a significant mentor for me as I seek to describe how the intergenerational legacy of lynching has been manifest in my own white family. From this mountain, beginning in the 1930s, Lillian Smith broke the codes of Southern white tradition by naming with unflinching and disloyal precision how lynching was used to terrorize Black people and keep white women in their place. Unlike many of her white contemporaries, Smith understood that racism and sexism were inextricably intertwined and that white women played a dual role as oppressor and oppressed.[1]

During my stay on Old Screamer Mountain, I wanted to study and write about the complex and contradictory role that white women played in the history of lynching. Black men and women were lynched as a means of terrorizing and exerting power over Black communities. It was also a way of consolidating white patriarchal control of white women's bodies and diverting attention from the physical and sexual assault that Black and white women routinely faced at the hands of white men. Despite popular notions to the contrary, white men were not the sole perpetrators and advocates of lynching. White women brought their children to lynchings, sometimes holding their little bodies high above the crowd for a better view of the desecrating, brutalizing violence.[2]

There were other white women who protested lynching and organized campaigns to abolish it, most notably the Association of Southern Women for the Prevention of Lynching (ASWPL), which was organized in 1930 and eventually boasted a membership of 4 million white women. Despite the important accomplishments of the ASWPL, its leaders routinely rejected overtures from Black women leaders to work collaboratively, and they vehemently opposed federal antilynching legislation and the suffrage of Black women. Ironically, the very white women who were passionately working to oppose racial violence engaged in racist hierarchies that ignored, dismissed, and excluded the leadership and concerns of Black women.[3]

As with so many other aspects of lynching, the role of white women in this heinous history has been largely repressed or ignored by contemporary white women. African American feminists such as Ida B. Wells-Barnett, bell hooks, Ruby Sales, and Emma Coleman Jordan have consistently challenged white women to own, face, and grapple with this critical part of our history.[4] Until we do, they warn, genuine bonds and collaboration between Black and white women will be impossible. Until we do, we will continue to reenact the dynamics and patterns that undergird contemporary white supremacy and racial violence. As Jordan states, "The paradox of feminist history is that lynching was used as a mechanism to control the social behavior and status of white women, and African-Americans—men and women, even as white women benefitted from their elevated position in the racial hierarchy built on lynching. Therefore, the first step across the river of blood between us requires identification of, and acceptance of the complex role white women played during the era of lynching."[5]

When I reserved my cabin at the Lillian Smith Center nearly one year earlier, I had no way of knowing that my stay there would coincide with the final days of the George Zimmerman trial. I had come to Georgia to read and write about the ideology that undergirded lynching, how it continues to infect white Americans, and why we must make this history visible. Every headline and news report about the trial confirmed the urgent need for this work. The politics, patterns, and policies of lynching were brazenly reproduced in that Sanford, Florida, courtroom.

Except for Trayvon Martin and George Zimmerman, the main players in this trial were white. Judge Debra Nelson, who presided over the case and made critical decisions that affected its outcome, was white. The entire prosecution team was white, with the possible exception of Special Prosecutor Angela Corey, a granddaughter of Syrian immigrants. Zimmerman's lawyers, Don West and Mark O'Mara, were white. Perhaps most disturbing and ominous of all, five of the six jurors were white women.

Race alone was not a fail-proof predictor of how individuals would approach this case or what the eventual outcome would be. As Justice Clarence Thomas proves, not all lawyers of color share an antiracist perspective. A white attorney who had done his or her own antiracist work through the years could have brought such a perspective. Furthermore, the structural racism that pervades the US judicial system is not merely the sum of the individuals present.

Nevertheless, I can imagine that Trayvon Martin's parents, Sybrina Fulton and Tracy Martin, were devastated, but not completely surprised, when this jury found George Zimmerman not guilty in the killing of their unarmed son. Long before the trial got underway, history was stacked against them.

The odds are tilted in favor of white shooters with Black victims in states with stand your ground laws such as Florida's. Furthermore, even in states without stand your ground laws, white people who kill Black people are far more likely to be found not guilty than the other way around.[6]

Before the trial got underway, Judge Nelson forbade the prosecution from speaking about racial profiling. Only the word *profiling* could be used.[7] Thus began the racial sanitizing. Even though the entire case was saturated with racism, the judge and attorneys agreed not to speak explicitly about race. Such a move raises the question of who benefits from silence about race, racism, and racial profiling. This prohibition mirrors common white refusals to admit to racism: that if race is not discussed, then racism is not in the room. And prohibitions like this force discussions of racism back onto people of color, who often get accused of "playing the race card" and "inserting race" into race-erased situations. The belief that not talking about racism creates and protects a level playing field is a fantasy constructed by white people who benefit every day from seeing themselves and each other as racially unmarked.

When I first heard about Judge Nelson's ruling that racial profiling could not be named in the prosecution's opening remarks, I assumed that the prosecution team fought back and argued that racial profiling was key to this case. Apparently, I was wrong. In a press conference held right after the verdict was announced, Angela Corey declared, "This case has never been about race or the right to bear arms. We believe this case all along was about boundaries, and George Zimmerman exceeded those boundaries."[8]

Whatever Corey's motivation for declaring that the case was never about race, her pronouncement represents a profound betrayal of Trayvon Martin and his parents. At their first public appearances after their son's death, Sybrina Fulton and Tracy Martin stated their unequivocal conviction that had their son been white, he would not have been targeted and killed by Zimmerman.

Angela Corey may have believed she could not win this case in the state of Florida by trying to prove racial profiling. But that is a different matter altogether. For her to state, in the face of Trayvon's grieving parents, that this case "has never been about race" is to pour salt in raw, open wounds. That Corey did not realize the offensiveness of her statement should give us all pause about how the prosecution's case was conceived and argued.

In a courtroom where mention of race was muzzled and stricken from the record, the defense team had a field day using race-baiting scare tactics at every turn. Not needing to use the R word, they did everything in their power to paint a portrait of Trayvon Martin that matched the all-too-common stereotype of a menacing, dangerous, gang-banging Black teenager. In rhetoric reminiscent of the language used to defend lynching for more than 150 years, the lawyers sought to convince the jurors that Trayvon Martin posed a mortal threat to them and their families. Charles Blow noted that the defense team utilized "old racial tropes" designed to evoke fear in the white female jurors: "for example, when the defense held up a picture of a shirtless Martin and told the jurors that this was the person Zimmerman encountered the night he shot him. But in fact it was not the way Zimmerman had seen Martin. Consciously or subconsciously, the defense played on an old racial trope: asking the all-female jury—mostly white—to fear the image of the glistening black buck, as Zimmerman had."[9] In his closing arguments, Zimmerman's attorney lugged in a large piece of heavy cement and stated that Trayvon Martin wasn't an unarmed teenager carrying just a bag of Skittles and a can of pop. "He had armed himself with the concrete sidewalk," O'Mara declared.

One might think that such a ludicrous argument would be dismissed by the jury as the posturing of a desperate attorney. How could a sidewalk be seen as a lethal weapon comparable to a loaded gun? Surely, the jurors wouldn't fall for such cheap theatrics. Problem was, the old racial tropes still have power precisely because the imprint of lynching continues to shape white feelings, stereotypes, assumptions, and fears about Black male bodies. The fact that the defense could only conjure up a nonsensical sidewalk as his weapon made no dent in the power of the old, racial story. Trayvon was judged to be armed, trespassing, and dangerous.

To find George Zimmerman guilty, the jurors needed to have the capacity to believe that Trayvon Martin could be a victim. Right there was the rub. In the day-to-day working of the criminal justice system, we have ample evidence that white people perceive Black males as victimizers. The recent statistics about police practices in New York City reveal this deep-seated, long-practiced bias. Thousands of innocent New Yorkers are stopped and frisked each year by the New York Police Department, the vast majority of those stopped being African American and Latino males.[10] As Marc Lamont Hill noted, from the moment he was killed, "Martin's identity and character were called into question by law enforcement, media, and everyday citizens in ways that transformed the 'Trial of George Zimmerman' into 'The Trial of Trayvon Martin.'"[11]

Justice for Trayvon Martin may have been doomed at the point of jury selection. I realize that the "jury of one's peers" in this case referred to George Zimmerman rather than Trayvon Martin. Nevertheless, I am puzzled as to why the prosecution allowed a jury of six women, five of whom are white. Even though Sanford County is 80 percent white, representation from the other 20 percent would certainly have been in order. I also wonder whether potential jurors of color were ruled out more quickly on the false presumption that they, not white people, are racially biased.

Three days after the verdict was announced on July 13, CNN correspondent Anderson Cooper obtained an exclusive interview with one of the white jurors.[12] Throughout the interview, she displayed sympathy for, and an identification with, the emotions and actions that led George Zimmerman to confront and ultimately kill Trayvon Martin. She acknowledged that she felt bad for Trayvon and his parents, sad for their loss, but she described George like she might describe a family member or friend: as a man "whose heart was in the right place" but "didn't use good judgment" because he was so justifiably concerned about crime in the neighborhood.

That level of empathy was never expressed for Trayvon. She regretted the loss of life, but she believed Trayvon was the aggressor who got mad and threw the first punch. She wished George hadn't gotten out of the car, but that didn't make him the aggressor; George "just got in a little bit too deep." Disavowing that race played any role in George's actions, she thought Trayvon's behavior warranted suspicion, especially considering all the break-ins that had occurred recently in the neighborhood. After all, she said, "it, being late at night, dark at night, raining, and anybody would think anybody walking down the road stopping and turning and looking... is suspicious."

Anderson Cooper didn't press her at this point and ask whether she believed George Zimmerman would have pursued a white teenager who was walking slowly in the rain at night. Would Zimmerman have gotten out of his car to follow him? Would Zimmerman have used words like "those punks... they always get away" if the teenager had been white? Cooper did not follow up with any of those questions.

Most disturbing was to hear this juror say that the issue of racial profiling never came up in their deliberations. Not once. When asked, she said she'd be happy to have George Zimmerman on a neighborhood watch in her community because she believes he has learned his lesson and won't go too far again.

When I consider the ways that the legacy of lynching is imprinted on white minds and imaginations, this juror displayed them: the lack of empathy for the Black victim, the disavowal that racism played any role in the violence, her belief that this particular man posed a danger to her and her (white) neighbors, the regret that things got "a bit out of hand," the conviction that the victim got what was coming to him. The specter of darkness, imminent threat, and danger—all associated with Black male bodies—are embedded in her assertion that killing was warranted: *it, being late at night, dark at night, raining, and anybody would think anybody walking down the road stopping and turning and looking... is suspicious.*

As if the verdict were not open to question, extremely painful, and even egregious to an entire segment of the American populace, the self-congratulatory speeches of the prosecuting team, after the verdict was announced, were surreal. The entirely white team of prosecuting attorneys gathered on a podium, and the state prosecutor, Angela Corey, began by saying, "We are so proud to stand before you."[13] Proud? George Zimmerman had just been found not guilty of murder. No word of regret about the verdict was expressed. No show of concern for the devastating impact this verdict had on the grieving parents of Trayvon Martin. Instead, Corey declared that the prosecutors in this trial "had shown respect for the living and had done their best to assure due process to all involved, and we believe we brought out the truth on behalf of Trayvon Martin." As though "bringing out the truth" was enough to render the "not guilty" verdict insignificant by comparison.

Like a celebrity at an Academy Awards ceremony where congratulations and heartfelt thanks are stated unendingly, the smiling special prosecutor said, "There are so many people to thank, starting with Sheriff Eslinger and his entire Sheriff's Office. They have been so good to us." On the heels of their failure to win a conviction, Corey talked about her "amazing team of lawyers and investigators," lauding their skill and prowess. The entire speech was about the goodness and virtue of the white people who had so selflessly given their time and talents to this case. In her entire four-minute speech, the name of Trayvon Martin was spoken one time. She didn't thank or even acknowledge Trayvon's parents. Instead, she focused on the judge and her fellow attorneys and investigators "who put their lives on hold."

Without expressing any judgment or regrets about their verdict, Corey showered praise on the jury who had displayed what she characterized as selfless sacrifice: "I want to thank the jury for the sixteen hours of deliberation that they took to go over all of the facts and circumstances.... They worked very hard. We honor them for their service." Again, not one word about the hours, days, and months of agony experienced by Trayvon's family leading up to this trial, to say nothing of the pain they endured having to listen to the defense team's accusation that their son was "responsible for his own death." Nor did Corey bother to mention the sixteen hours of torture it must have been for Sybrina Fulton and Tracy Martin to wait, hoping against hope that the jury would do the right thing and find Trayvon's killer guilty of murder.

In fact, Corey never spoke the names of Trayvon's parents or addressed them directly in her speech. She gave them a passing nod, almost as an afterthought, when saying, "And, of course, our hearts as always go out to our victim's family and to all victims of crime." Sybrina Fulton and Tracy Martin were rendered invisible in her remarks, lumped together with "all victims of crime."

When Corey relinquished the microphone to her colleague, Bernie de la Rionda, he began by thanking the media for respecting their privacy and then said, "I am disappointed as we are with the verdict, but we accept it." That was the first and only expression of disappointment from the entire team. Clearly, de la Rionda didn't want to linger on any aspect of the trial that would signal negativity. He went on to praise the "great criminal justice system in this country...the best in the world."

Attorney John Guy was a man of few words: "We have from the beginning just prayed for the truth to come out and for peace to be the result. And that continues to be our prayers, and we believe they have been answered."

By the time the fourth and last prosecutor, Richard Mantei, came to the microphone, it became clear what was at the heart of this orchestrated ceremony. Each of the four attorneys was bent on assuring us that "the truth has been served" and the United States has the greatest criminal justice system in the world. Under and between their words lay this subtext: We should all just calm down, accept what has happened, and make sure that peace prevails in the streets. These white lawyers clearly feared that violence might erupt in reaction to the verdict. They were seeking to exonerate themselves preemptively by reassuring everyone they had done the best they could.

Like the others, Mantei didn't voice regret or remorse about the verdict. Instead, he lauded "the parents of the dead teenage victim, Trayvon Martin," for handling a difficult situation "like ladies and gentlemen," displaying "class," and "keeping their pain in check when they needed to." As the last speaker of this all-white team of attorneys, he too was invoking the need to keep the peace by lifting Trayvon's parents up as a model for others about how to stay calm and not make a scene.

It was a solidly white narrative from beginning to end. No place for grief. No room for outrage. Everything is as it should be. The truth has been served. The jury did the best they could. Our criminal justice system has proven once again that it works. Everyone can go home now, assured that the world has not ended. Life goes on.

And you bet it does for those of us who are white. When the verdict was announced, life was not altered one iota for white people in this country. They are no less safe because of it. The verdict does not place their children's lives in jeopardy.

In the aftermath of the verdict, several of my white feminist friends posted their outrage on Facebook, expressing shock and dismay that a jury of six women would exonerate George Zimmerman. "Why couldn't those women in the jury feel identification with Sybrina Fulton?" they asked. "Why didn't sisterhood or mother love trump racism in their deliberations?"

Legally speaking, the critical issue in this trial was that the jury could not feel identification with Sybrina's son, Trayvon; could not see him as an unarmed victim of murder. I believe this lack of identification has its roots, in part, in the legacies of lynching that continue to infect white Americans. Furthermore, the history of white feminist movements reveals that racism is not that easily trumped, and the betrayal of Black women by white women far more commonplace than not. The horrific history of lynching that occurred during the nineteenth and twentieth centuries has effectively been expunged from the collective memory of white people. And too few white feminist organizations have addressed the continuing realities of police brutality, mass incarceration, and racial violence in a systematic, sustained, and collaborative fashion. Racism will continue to trump sisterhood unless and until those of us who are white and feminist critically examine what Emma Coleman Jordan calls "the bloody legacy upon which" our own power exists.[14]

If we do not examine and address the ways this bloody history continues to shape our imaginations, actions, policies, and priorities, it will be tragically replicated again and again as it was in the lynching of Trayvon Martin and the exoneration of his killer.

16

At the Hands of Persons Unknown

THE VERDICT IN THE MICHAEL BRELO CASE

I could not turn away or close my eyes as I watched the verdict in the Michael Brelo case being rendered by Judge P. O'Donnell in Cleveland on May 23, 2015.[1] The nearly hour-long justification for exonerating Officer Brelo on all counts was bone chilling to behold. In every respect, it amounted to a judicial justification for state-sanctioned lynching. I don't use the word *lynching* metaphorically. I use it because so many of the characteristics of historical lynching are replicated in this case.

Lynching can be defined as an extrajudicial killing by a group of people who seek to punish an alleged transgressor and/or intimidate a minority group. Between 1877 and 1950, nearly four thousand men and women were lynched by white people in America, and the vast majority of the victims were Black.[2] The alleged crimes often proved to be unfounded, and the punishments inflicted in these acts of racial terror were diabolically brutalizing in their use of excessive force. Nevertheless, the white instigators and witnesses believed the punishment was justified because of their judgment that the victim posed an imminent threat.

Even though hundreds, if not thousands, of white people witnessed lynchings, only an infinitesimal number of perpetrators were ever arrested, much less convicted. The so-called investigations by law enforcement officials always resulted in the same verdict: The lynching occurred "at the hands of persons unknown."[3]

No one was held accountable. The message to white America was clear: You may perpetrate these horrific acts with impunity.

Let's review the facts of the case against Officer Brelo. In November 2012, a car with two Black passengers—Timothy Russell and Malissa Williams—backfired. Police mistook the backfire for a gunshot, which resulted in a twenty-two-mile chase that involved more than one hundred officers and speeds of over a hundred miles an hour. That chase ended in a school parking lot where thirteen officers, Brelo being one of them, riddled the car and the bodies of Russell and Williams with a total of 137 rounds. Officer Brelo fired forty-nine of those rounds after exiting his car. Midway in his firing, he jumped onto the hood of the car and shot downward into the car's windshield at least fifteen times. The officers later testified that they believed the occupants were armed, but no gun was found in the car.[4]

Officer Brelo was found not guilty by Judge O'Donnell on the charge of manslaughter (knowingly causing the deaths of Timothy Russell and Malissa Williams) and the lesser charge of felonious assault. Regarding manslaughter, Judge O'Donnell concluded that it was impossible to determine definitively which bullets proved to be the lethal "straw that broke the camel's back" (yes, he used that phrase).[5]

In effect, Judge O'Donnell declared that the deaths of Timothy Russell and Malissa Williams occurred at the hands of persons unknown.

Regarding felonious assault, Judge O'Donnell concurred with the defense that, even though one hundred rounds had already been fired into the car, Officer Brelo was justified in firing from the hood of the car because he had "an objectively reasonable perception that the Malibu and its inhabitants posed an imminent threat to him and the other officers."

How in the world could it be reasonable that two people trapped in a car, surrounded by thirteen officers who had fired one hundred rounds, still posed an imminent threat? Judge O'Donnell offered these explanations:

- Brelo had heard other officers shout that the occupants probably had loaded weapons.
- Russell had traveled over a hundred miles an hour during the chase, ignoring traffic lights, and had slammed into a police car in the parking lot.

- By the end of the chase, Brelo was in a part of the city "unfamiliar to him," and the entrance to the parking lot was a "dusty, dirty area" obscuring his vision.
- Brelo thought he saw both people in the car holding something black in their hands.
- Brelo acted in difficult conditions, with flashing lights and gunfire, which he described as "worse than being under attack from rockets and mortars while serving as a Marine in Iraq."[6]

Although Judge O'Donnell acknowledged that it was by then known there was no gun in the car and Officer Brelo was mistaken about the origin of the gunshots, he declared, "it is Brelo's perception of a threat that matters."[7] And that perception was justified because "the car was still running and to Brelo's observation the occupants were still moving." In effect, Judge O'Donnell blamed the victims for their own deaths and exonerated Officer Brelo's irrational fear and excessive use of violence.

How long will we as a nation allow this state-sanctioned violence to continue unchecked? How often must we witness perpetrators being exonerated while the unarmed victims are found guilty of being Black? How much proof does white America require to recognize that our justice system needs radical transformation—so that chokeholds, shooting fleeing suspects in the back, and firing 137 rounds into a parked car will no longer be sanctioned as a "constitutionally reasonable response"?

Once again, in Cleveland, the legacy of lynching was made manifest. Once again, no law enforcement officer was held accountable for an unspeakably excessive use of force in the deaths of unarmed Black citizens. Once again, the message to police officers is clear: You may perpetrate these horrific acts with impunity.

17

"The Fierce Urgency of Now"

This essay, written in April 2017, commemorates the fiftieth anniversary of Dr. Martin Luther King Jr.'s sermon, "Beyond Vietnam: A Time to Break Silence," preached in April 1967.

We are now faced with the fact, my friends, that tomorrow is today. We are confronted with the fierce urgency of now. In this unfolding conundrum of life and history, there is such a thing as being too late. Procrastination is still the thief of time. Life often leaves us standing bare, naked, and dejected with a lost opportunity.... We may cry out desperately for time to pause in her passage, but time is adamant to every plea and rushes on. Over the bleached bones and jumbled residues of numerous civilizations are written the pathetic words, "Too late." There is an invisible book of life that faithfully records our vigilance or our neglect. —DR. MARTIN LUTHER KING JR., "Beyond Vietnam," 1967

Fifty years ago, Dr. Martin Luther King Jr. declared in the pulpit at Riverside Church in New York City that the war in Vietnam was "a symptom of a far deeper malady within the American spirit." Dr. King warned that America would continue to be a dangerous purveyor of oppressive, counterrevolutionary violence in distant lands if it failed to acknowledge the systemic racism that lay—as an unhealed wound—at the heart of our nation. He decried the egregious irony that young Black men were being sent eight thousand miles away "to guarantee liberties in Southeast Asia which they had not found in southwest Georgia and East Harlem."[1]

With prophetic urgency, Dr. King declared, "We are confronted with the fierce urgency of now.... We may cry out desperately for time to pause in her passage, but time is adamant to every plea and rushes on."

It would surely grieve Dr. King that fifty years after he delivered that impassioned plea, every major institution in the United States is still rife with racial disparities and inequities. It would grieve him that racism continues to exact a devastating toll on communities of color through state-sanctioned violence, staggering unemployment, redlining, health care disparities, and mass incarceration.

In that Riverside sermon, delivered on April 4, 1967, Dr. King issued another grave warning: "There is an invisible book of life that faithfully records our vigilance or our neglect."

In the fifty years since, I fear that this invisible book of life has recorded far more deeds of neglect than vigilance by those of us who are white Americans; far more deeds of silent acquiescence than outrage, remorse, or reparation. Fifty years after Dr. King sought to rouse our sustained indignation about racial violence, unarmed men, women, and children continue to be racially profiled, stopped, frisked, thrown to the ground, choked, and killed. Invariably, grand juries that investigate this state-sanctioned violence fail to indict the white officers who claimed they had good reason "to fear for their lives."

When will those of us who are white recognize the fierce urgency of now? When will we demand a truthful accounting of who is actually in mortal danger in this country?

When will we grapple with the stark truth that Ta-Nehisi Coates wrote in a letter to his fifteen-year-old son? "Here is what I would like you to know: In America, it is traditional to destroy the black body—*it is heritage*."[2]

How many Black men, women, and children have to die a death at the hands of police before those of us who are white bring our collective hearts, minds, and souls to the task of excavating, naming, and untying the lethal knot that remains endemic in white imaginations?

This lethal knot has many threads—each one a legacy and manifestation of white supremacy. Threads of fear of Black bodies. Threads of contempt for Black bodies. Threads of rage at so-called insubordination. Threads of feeling powerless while we wield structural power. Threads of feeling small even when we're armed with assault weapons.

We heard this lethal legacy of fear in the testimony of Officer Darren Wilson in Ferguson, Missouri. Michael Brown was an unarmed Black teenager, no taller than Wilson, when the officer shot Brown six times before killing him in August 2014. But the grand jury failed to indict Wilson after he testified, "When I grabbed [Michael Brown] the only way I can describe it is I felt like a five-year-old holding onto Hulk Hogan.... That's how big he felt and how small I felt just from grasping his arm."[3]

We witnessed white rage at so-called insubordination when a Texas patrolman stopped Sandra Bland for failing to signal a lane change. After Bland dared suggest that she was being targeted for no reason except her race, the patrolman pulled her from the car, threw her face down to the ground, and pinned her with his knee while handcuffing her.[4]

It is not the work of people of color to unearth, unravel, and exorcize this lethal knot of white supremacist consciousness that remains so deeply rooted in the white psyche. This is white people's work. We must engage this deep work in every relationship and vocation at our disposal—as parents, friends, coworkers, neighbors, and citizens of this nation.

If we fail to do this urgent work, white demagogues will continue to step into the breach, misname the mortal danger, shore up the guns and tanks, and stoke the lethal fear with terrifying and terrorizing consequences. As Dr. King declared fifty years ago: "We are now faced with the fact, my friends, that tomorrow is today. We are confronted with the fierce urgency of now. In this unfolding conundrum of life and history, there is such a thing as being too late."

IV. STAYING POWER

18

What Will It Take for White People to Stay the Course?

After the brutal, suffocating murder of George Floyd on May 25, 2020, millions of Americans took to the streets, voicing their grief and rage about the killing by police of unarmed Black people. Predominantly young demonstrators, many of whom were white, called on the nation to recognize and mend the deep racial disparities in education, health care, employment, housing, and policing. For weeks on end, demonstrations continued in cities and towns across the nation. By July 1, 2020, polls estimated that 15 to 20 million Americans had demonstrated, making those protests the largest in American history.[1]

Also, in the wake of Floyd's death, promises to address and rectify racial inequities were announced by corporations, universities, and the National Football League. The American Academy of Pediatrics, American Medical Association, and American College of Physicians declared racism a public health issue and called for an end to police brutality against Black Americans. Organizations specializing in diversity, equity, and inclusion (DEI) trainings were inundated with requests from businesses, educational institutions, and nonprofits seeking DEI workshops and coaching.

In response to these numbers and promises issued by high-profile companies, media pundits repeatedly asked, "Could this be a tipping point? Could it be that fundamental and sweeping changes are occurring?"

Conjectures such as these were understandable, but considering what has transpired since 2020, we learned once again that massive demonstrations alone do not create tipping points. Substantive and sustainable changes are forged by people who commit to the long-haul work of racial justice, equity, and repair. Black, Indigenous, and other people of color (BIPOC) could count on the fact that even if the summer of 2020 was a tipping point, the journey ahead would be a long one. What they could not count on was the staying power of the white people who took to the streets with fervent urgency. As Charles McKinney, chair of Africana Studies at Rhodes College in Tennessee noted, "Historically, when we see higher levels of participation from white folks in movements and moments like this, that participation falls off precipitously after we move away from the protest."[2]

It has happened far too often that white people are jolted awake, feel deep indignation, become engaged, and then check out again, fall back into familiar routines, and retreat from the long-haul work of justice making. This all-too-predictable pattern caused Hakeem Jefferson, political scientist at Stanford University, to doubt that the 2020 protest signified a watershed moment in white Americans' lives: "All of these white people on the front lines of these protests go back to their white neighborhoods and their overwhelmingly white and better schools. They protest alongside [Black people], but they don't live alongside them. As much as people really want that progress narrative, I don't think it exists yet."[3]

By the fall of 2020, white supremacist backlash was on the rise, and well-funded campaigns sought to restrict the teaching of so-called divisive concepts such as systemic racism, critical race theory, intersectionality, and white privilege. On September 28, 2020, then-President Trump issued Executive Order 13950, which banned federal agencies, contractors, and grant recipients from providing DEI trainings that analyzed and addressed systemic racism. In the following months, this restrictive campaign spread to state legislatures and local school boards. By February 2023, thirty-five states had introduced 137 bills "limiting what schools can teach with regard to race, American history, politics, sexual orientation and gender identity."[4]

Despite the chilling effect of these campaigns on public school educators and the failure of many corporations to enact the sweeping reforms they promised, Princeton professor Keeanga-Yamahtta Taylor argues that the magnitude of the 2020 protests should not be underestimated.[5] Those protests graphically demonstrated that a growing number of Americans have come to believe that racism is systemic in nature and not simply synonymous with personal prejudice. According to Taylor, "we should recognize how much the conversation has changed. There is now widespread agreement that racism has been embedded in the public and private institutions that govern our lives and dictate our access to services, justifying the demands for specific actions to undo the harmful results."

The far right fears this changing narrative. The stated pretext for banning books and prohibiting the teaching of subjects such as slavery and African American history is to protect white children from discomfort and psychological distress. But I suspect the deeper trepidation is what they beheld in the summer of 2020, namely solidarity between white, Black, and Brown young people. As Keeanga-Yamahtta Taylor put it, "The invented crisis of critical race theory is also intended to sow tension and suspicion among those who have an interest in solidarity and connection."[6]

Reflecting on the protests in 2020 and the campaigns that seek to sow tension and suspicion, I believe it is imperative that those of us who are white wrestle with questions such as these:

What will it take for those of us who are white to understand that the work of racial justice is a marathon, not a sprint?

How will we develop the consciousness, commitment, and resiliency to stay the course and not check out?

What's it going to take?

White people who strive to become antiracist allies, and embody the solidarity needed to dismantle systemic racism, must be willing to engage in strenuous and persistent work. We need to develop new muscles and unwavering commitment if we seek to be cocreators of the tipping points. Here's how I would describe some of the dimensions of that lifelong work.

1. Understand That Racism Is Far More Than Personal Prejudice

Time and again, I have witnessed multiracial conversations, and efforts to work together across race, flounder or fall apart because white people and people of color have profoundly divergent associations with the words *racism* and *racist*. It is as if we are speaking different languages.

For many white people, the word *racism* is associated with individual prejudicial attitudes or behaviors. And the word *racist* conjures up images of hateful behaviors perpetrated by overtly bigoted individuals like white nationalists and

Ku Klux Klan members. In other words—those people, not us. That accounts for the defensiveness that so frequently surfaces as white people insist that they are not racist, and that racism could not have been at play if they were involved in the situation.

When BIPOC speak of racism, they are referring to something far more encompassing than individual attitudes or behaviors. They are testifying to their lived experience of a pervasive reality that is systemic and multilayered, with deep historical roots and manifest in every level of American society—personal, interpersonal, institutional, and cultural. They are talking about a system of advantage based on race.

In every era of American history, this white supremacist system has advantaged white people and disinherited people of color: in the theft of Indigenous land and in residential boarding schools; in the enslavement of Black people lasting 246 years; in the convict lease system that reenslaved Black people after emancipation; in lynching and other forms of Jim Crow terrorism; in immigration quotas and periodic mass deportations of Asian and Latinx communities; in denying people of color access to mortgages when the Federal Housing Administration was established in the 1930s; in the internment of Japanese Americans in the 1940s; in denying voting rights and access to fair housing to African Americans; in the spike of hate crimes and discrimination perpetrated against Arab Americans since 9/11.

We cannot understand who and where we are as a nation today if we do not know this history because every major institution in the United States is still rife with racial disparities and inequities. It is my conviction that the soul-splitting legacies engendered by generations of white supremacy and enslavement remain largely unacknowledged, unhealed, deeply rooted, and endemic in our white psyches with terrifying, terrorizing consequences. Until the psychic, emotional, and spiritual legacies of this shameful history are acknowledged and confronted, white Americans will continue to project (consciously or unconsciously) racialized fears, fantasies, rage, and scapegoating onto people of color.

2. Understand the Unearned Privileges We Are Granted

One meaning of being white is that we are granted unearned privileges and structural power simply by reason of our race. Regardless of our best intentions, we are granted exemptions, entitlements, and privileges denied BIPOC. White people are not racially profiled or routinely followed by security guards in stores. We do not have to produce ID and explain where we are going when walking, biking, or driving. We do not face higher insurance or mortgage rates by reason of our skin color. We are not called upon to speak for other members of our race. Unless we have Black or Brown children, we do not have to engage in the tense yet necessary conversation with our kids about staying safe while interacting with police.

Peggy McIntosh has noted that "privilege is a fugitive subject" about which white people were meant to remain oblivious.[7] Making privilege visible to ourselves and to other white people demands constant vigilance. But it is our work. It is not the work of BIPOC to educate white people about privilege. We must do it. It is important to do because it interrupts the dominant narrative that blames people of color for the gross inequities in our society.

One way we can better understand how unearned privileges have been passed down to us over the course of many generations is by engaging in what Aurora Levins Morales calls "radical genealogy"—the practice of learning about our ancestors by investigating the historical context in which they lived and asking how race and class were at play in their lives.[8]

Radical genealogy can make structural privilege visible in a very personal way, as in the case of Sarah Browning. In an article titled "A Crime Against Humanity Sent Me to Harvard," Browning explains how she inherited intergenerational wealth that began with her great-grandfather, who was born into an enslaving family in Virginia. "Let me say it plainly," Sarah Browning writes. "The unpaid labor of black people sent me to Harvard."[9]

Asked why she felt compelled to investigate and write about this ancestral inheritance, Browning said, "[If] we don't face that history squarely—and acknowledge the ways it still distorts the structure of our society today—we'll be incapable of undoing its legacy. White people will continue to believe that the extreme race-based wealth gap in this country has other causes—that they somehow deserve advantages denied to others based on their skin color."

White privilege cannot be given away, but we can interrupt the habits, practices, and policies that keep it in place. One of those habits is the sense of entitlement to make decisions for everyone without consulting those most affected by our decisions.[10]

3. Cultivate Spaces Where We Can Access and Express Fear, Shame, and Grief

For white people, the process of understanding, claiming, and embodying an antiracist identity is not just cognitive work. It is also heart and soul work. Beneath the intellectual grasp of issues, there often lies a terror in white people of being found wanting. If those of us who are white do not dive deep and excavate the fears that hold us hostage, we will come into racially diverse settings holding back, walking on eggshells, intensely self-conscious, fearful about making mistakes or, worse yet, being seen as racist.

Latina educator and author Lillian Roybal Rose describes it this way: "For People of Color, an encounter with a white person who knows what is right but has not processed it emotionally can be frustrating and exhausting. Every word, every signal breeds confusion. Whites busily guarding a politically correct posture are impossible to reach on a human level, because they have an image to protect."[11]

Shame, pain, and anger are closely related emotions that surface when those of us who are white awaken to the realities of historic and contemporary racism. In those first stages of waking up, we discover how much we did not learn, did not know, did not recognize, and did not feel. The systemic nature of racism and white privilege effectively anesthetizes white people against feeling the pain of racism.

Unfortunately, too many of us get stuck in self-deprecation or shame because we are not willing to risk the long road of reclamation, the road of reclaiming pieces of ourselves that have been numbed, cut off, and lost through the intergenerational legacies of racism and white supremacy. We need to feel, claim, and give voice to our grief, distress, and rage at racism. And it is best if we do that with each other so that our emotional work does not distract or disrupt the collaborative work we need to do with people of color. For example, white people often seek forgiveness from people of color as they awaken to the harm that they or their ancestors wreaked, but this request can be toxic for BIPOC because it shifts focus from their experience of racism to our need for validation.

The work of accessing fear, shame, and grief does not end with hearing each other's pain. That pain needs to give way to something deeper if we are serious about confronting racism. As Nancy Richardson has stated, if white people do not move beyond "a vague sense of dis-ease," they will continue to exhibit symptoms that "run the gamut from denial to guilt, from arrogance to self-pity, from defensiveness to passivity."

> Without tools for accurate diagnosis of the disease, appropriate steps toward health are impossible. In order to develop these tools, it is essential that we as white people learn to understand the history of this country and our place in it, that we recognize ways in which we collaborate with white supremacist policies and practices, that we develop communities of resistance, and that we participate in collaborative strategies for transfor-

mation. In order to do this, we need to be honest with each other, to avoid self-righteousness, to provide mutual self-criticism without succumbing to self-pity or guilt-tripping, and to receive challenge from colleagues as evidence of support.[12]

4. Take Action to Interrupt Racism in the Interpersonal and Institutional Realms

In the interpersonal realm, we can interrupt racism by speaking up and speaking out when white friends, family, or coworkers utter racist comments. Far too often, we fall silent in all-white settings, grateful no people of color were present to be harmed by what was said. But all of us should be angry when racism is uttered. The violence of demeaning speech does not just disappear. It is normalized by silence and assent. And it can take root in young people who witness it.

With trusted friends, we can learn and practice the skills of interrupting the racism we witness. We can also name and examine what lies behind our silence when racist behaviors and policies are at play, such as failure to recognize the offense, fear of publicly humiliating the offender, fear of jeopardizing our rank or reputation in an organization, inability to formulate an adequate response, or fear of doing more harm than good if we speak up. Accessing our distress at racism and channeling that distress into useful interventions are critically important skills for white people to learn and practice.

We can also interrupt racism in the interpersonal realm by examining the impact our words and behaviors have had. When confronted by people of color, or other white people, about harm we have inflicted, it is natural to invoke our good intentions with, "Oh, I think you misunderstood me," or "That isn't what I intended to say."

Defensiveness about good intentions can also get expressed by shutting down, sulking, crying, or minimizing. Other white people often rush to defend us, declaring things like, "Oh, you've misunderstood my friend. I've known her for years. She doesn't have a racist bone in her body!" Whatever way we express defensiveness, we are pleading innocence, claiming the right to absolve ourselves, and refusing to confront the harm we caused.

This flight into defensiveness and good intentions can be all too frequent, but we do not have to stay stuck there. We can learn how to stay present, and we can learn from the challenge by practicing other behaviors: By listening rather than reacting. By honoring the fact that the person who has challenged us has been authentic with us when expressing their pain or anger. By recognizing that this is a moment when our worldview could be deepened and expanded. By refraining from stealing the emotional center through tears and other emotional outbursts. By taking the anger of people of color seriously without always taking it personally. By not prematurely asking for forgiveness but rather asking ourselves, "What can I learn from this feedback and how might I do it differently next time?" By focusing more on the impact of our words and behaviors than on our intentions.

In the institutional realm, it is tempting to become overwhelmed by the enormity of systemic racism and feel very small and powerless in relation to it. But each one of us has spheres of influence in our lives—family; neighborhood; the places where we study, work, or volunteer; friendship circles; faith communities; or organizational affiliations. These are contexts where we can use our agency, voice, relationships, and resources to work collaboratively with others to bring about change.

For example, those of us who are parents have multiple, intersecting spheres of influence related to our children: the schools they attend, sports teams, parent-teacher associations—to name just a few. We can exercise significant agency and influence in those spheres of influence, asking critical questions about what our children are being exposed to. Do their history lessons include in-depth examination of how race, racism, and racial justice were at play in different historical eras? Are they being assigned literature written by authors of color? Are their teachers receiving in-depth and ongoing professional development related to cultural proficiency and racial justice? Do the schools our children attend have sports teams with names and mascots like the Chieftains, the Braves, or the Hurons? When students are the target of racial bullying or hate speech, are there mechanisms for constructive intervention, education, and resolution? What is the data in our school district about discipline and suspensions? How does that data reflect racial disparities?

If we do not know the answer to those questions, that is a place to start. We need to find out, and when we have discovered significant gaps in our children's education, seek out other parents who share our concerns and start organizing for change.

If our local school board has banned books or restricted the teaching of subjects such as the history of Indigenous dispossession and the enslavement of African Americans, we can reach out to parents who are equally concerned about these school board decisions. We can organize a group of concerned parents to draft a petition for the school board or attend school board meetings to voice our objections to the policies that have been enacted.

And in our homes, how are we as white parents initiating conversations with our children about racism-related events in our community, state, and nation?

There is so much work to be done, and there are so many silences to be broken in white communities. Spheres of influence in white communities are places where we need to show up, speak up, do serious racism inventories, and help organize for change.

5. Move Out of Social Segregation

Developing relationships of accountability with BIPOC is critically important, and it necessitates moving out of social segregation. To move out of social segregation and develop relationships with people of color means moving our white bodies into spaces we might not normally go. It means attending cultural, educational, or religious events that are organized by BIPOC. It means becoming involved in organizations where we are not in control. It means actively seeking out and listening to feedback from people of color. It means becoming engaged in antiracist organizations led by BIPOC. It means learning about the work for racial justice that people of color have undertaken, the setbacks they have suffered, and the victories they have won.

If we are affiliated with predominantly white organizations, we can shift the questions we ask when evaluating their programs. Rather than ask, "Why aren't more people of color attending our programs and projects?," we can ask, "When was the last time we attended programs and projects generated and led by people of color?" Rather than ask, "Where are they? Why aren't they here?," we can ask, "Where are we? Why aren't we there? Why aren't we actively making connections with Black, Indigenous, and other communities of color, becoming involved in organizations and movements that are led by BIPOC, respecting the priorities they identify as strategies for change, and sustaining our engagement over time?"

6. Nurture Truth-Telling Relationships of Support and Accountability

I doubt that we will develop the new muscles and resilience necessary to stay the course as antiracist white people if we fail to develop truth-telling relationships of support and accountability.

In 1992, Lynnette Stallworth, an African American friend and colleague, invited me to codesign and cofacilitate an eight-month antiracism seminar for

Black and white women called Difficult Conversations. I was deeply honored to be invited, and I did not realize how much I needed to learn. I assumed that my experience leading seminars on other topics would stand me in good stead for helping to design Difficult Conversations. Because I had created many flyers and brochures for those seminars, I presumed I would whip off one for Difficult Conversations.

I sent my draft to Lynnette, assuming she would be delighted that I had undertaken that initial step in our design process. When I received her response, I was taken aback and frankly irritated that she returned the flyer with words crossed out, question marks in the margins, phrases substituted, and a note attached that said, "This flyer may speak to white women but if you want Black women to attend, it has to be completely rewritten."

Together we rewrote that flyer. It was hard, time-consuming work to negotiate the wording, and I thought to myself, *What have I gotten myself into? This is only the flyer!*

After that preliminary work together, Lynnette phoned me and said, "Melanie, we need to slow down. I think it would be morally indefensible for us to invite Black and white women to dive deep and go places in this seminar where you and I have not yet gone with each other."

Lynnette and I postponed the seminar and met regularly over the course of a whole year for study, self-reflection, dialogue, and difficult conversations before we launched the seminar. It was a life-giving, life-changing year for me when I learned how critically important it is to cultivate truth-telling relationships of support and accountability.

By truth-telling relationships, I mean relationships where there is a shared commitment to hear each other *all the way through*, no matter how uncomfortable the speaking and the hearing may make us, and a shared commitment to holding each other's pain, anger, and joy. By support and accountability, I mean a shared commitment to help each other understand things we cannot, by ourselves, understand. James Baldwin said it like this: "If I love you, I have to make you conscious of the things you don't see."[13]

We will not do these truth-telling relationships perfectly. We are bound to disappoint each other at times. But I also know from experience that this kind of authenticity can be practiced and learned if we give ourselves to it. For example, we can practice humility, openness, and resiliency of spirit, learning that when we are challenged on our racism, we can find the grace to say, "I understand now why that remark, behavior, or program was racist. And because I understand now, I want to do it differently."

These relationships of accountability and support are not to be dabbled in. We must be strong and vulnerable enough to bring our whole selves to these relationships. In so doing, we always risk having our feelings hurt and our lives disrupted. But the potential for harm is far greater if we fail to take that risk.[14] How else are we going to develop the emotional, physical, and spiritual strength needed to become what the Rev. Dr. Ruby Sales calls "long-distance runners for justice"?

If you have been a jogger or a runner who has entertained the thought of doing a marathon or half-marathon, you know you cannot just wake up one morning with that thought, roll out of bed, put on your running shoes, and head to the marathon. It takes months, sometimes years, of practice and gaining strength.

I have never run a marathon, or had the ambition to do so, but I walk vigorously for an hour each morning. Over the years, it has been very helpful to have a walking partner who holds me to this discipline even when I am not feeling up to it. It is like that with my truth-telling friends who are passionate about racial justice. I do not know who I would be without them. They are the people I call when something occurs that I find upsetting. I check in with one of those friends, asking if I am overreacting. When they say "no," I seek their help in finding the words and the courage to make my voice heard.

7. Nurture Communities Where We Find Strength for the Long Haul

To sustain a lifelong commitment to racial justice requires an infusion of spirit and courage. Movements for racial justice have long been sustained by songs of struggle and hope, poetry, meditation, and remembering those who have gone before us and on whose shoulders we stand.

As Alice Walker has stated, "To acknowledge our ancestors means we are aware that we did not make ourselves, that the line stretches all the way back, perhaps, to God; or to Gods. We remember them because it is an easy thing to forget: that we are not the first to suffer, rebel, fight, love, and die. The grace with which we embrace life, in spite of the pain, the sorrows, is always a measure of what has gone before."[15]

We need to nurture spaces where we can gather to lament, rage, and grieve the defeats and setbacks we experience in the work for racial justice because there will be many. We also need spaces where we can gather to sing, laugh, rejoice, and celebrate the victories.

Amid struggle and self-scrutiny, there must be moments for beauty, tenderness, humor, and celebration. Otherwise, it becomes only grim duty, and we become strangers to ourselves, cut off from revitalizing power. One of the challenges of being, and staying, human is to take life seriously without taking ourselves too seriously. When we are no longer surprised by joy, it is a sure sign that our best intentions and good causes have gone sour.

Joy is not something we can plan, organize, create, or demand. It can only be received and savored or passed by and lost. If we are going to stay the course, it is imperative that we nurture communities where we can tenderly care for each other and celebrate even the smallest breakthroughs with joyful exuberance.

8. Be Able to Articulate the Personal Stake We Have in Ending Racism

On the first night of Doing Our Own Work: An Antiracism Seminar for White People, participants are invited to share what inspired them to enroll in this intensive, six-day experience. In one of the Doing Our Own Work seminars I cofacilitated, a woman I will call "Margaret" introduced herself with these words:

> I am here because it's time, long past time. I'm here because this is where I need to be. I work every day with colleagues of color. We rub shoulders, we attend staff meetings, plan events together, and commiserate about the future of our organization, but we don't deeply engage each other. It's like we live alongside each other. My colleagues of color are not guests in my home. I'm not a guest in theirs. We don't turn to each other to share our deepest grief or joy. The separation may look different than it did a hundred years ago, or forty years ago, or even twenty, but it is real. I am here because I want to examine my part in that separation. My fear of doing or saying the wrong thing. And my lack of awareness about the racism they face. I am here because I long for healing and wholeness. And I long to become more deeply engaged.

At the close of the first two days of Doing Our Own Work, Margaret shared with the group that she had come to see with greater clarity how she, as a white woman, could use her voice, her personal agency, and her resources to make a difference. She also expressed that she had moved from seeing racial justice as someone else's issue to claiming it as her own. "The fear has not disappeared," she said, "but I leave knowing that fear will no longer deter me from doing this sacred work."

The shift that Margaret described is a crucial change that white people need to undergo if we are going to move from being concerned about racism to being passionately invested in the work of racial justice. Often, those of us who are white begin grappling with the reality of systemic racism by thinking that racism is primarily a people of color issue and not fundamentally about us. We come to antiracism trainings and conferences thinking we are coming for the sake of our friends and colleagues of color or for family members of color who have been adopted or married into our families.

Showing up out of solidarity with BIPOC is critically important and necessary, but there is an essential shift that happens when white people discover that our lives, our souls, and the healing of our people also depend on the eradication of racism. Racism does not oppress us as white people, but racism has shaped and damaged us in myriad ways. It distorts the world we live in; teaches us lies about ourselves and our families; imbues us with a fear of difference that is ungrounded, misplaced, and irrational. We have inherited a racist legacy of silence, looking away, pretending not to notice, and numbness to the pain.

Until those of us who are white are able to own and claim the stake we have in ending racism, we will come and go, showing up for an antiracism workshop today, a demonstration tomorrow, then putting this issue aside the day after tomorrow, having decided that other issues demand our attention. Racial justice will remain one of many topics for socially conscious white people until we grasp that it is core to every other issue in this nation, and core to how we move in the world.

9. Forge New Ways of Being White in the World

In 1963, James Baldwin wrote these prophetic words in *The Fire Next Time*:

> A vast amount of energy that goes into the Negro problem is produced by the white man's profound desire not to be judged by those who are not white, not to be seen as he is, and at the same time a vast amount of white anguish is rooted in the white man's equally profound need to be seen as he is, to be released from the tyranny of his mirror. All of us know, whether or not we are able to admit it, that mirrors can only lie, that death by drowning is all that awaits one there. It is for this reason that love is so desperately sought and so cunningly avoided. Love takes off the masks that we fear we cannot live without and know we cannot live within. I use the word "love" here not merely in the personal sense but as a state of being, or a state of grace—not in the infantile American

sense of being made happy but in the tough and universal sense of quest and daring and growth.[16]

I believe it will be impossible for those of us who are white to develop the consciousness, commitment, and resiliency to stay the course and not check out if we cannot come to the work of racial justice from a place of self-love.[17] I am not referring to love in the sense of narcissistic self-focus and preoccupation, but rather, as James Baldwin says, "in the tough sense of quest and daring and growth."

If we cannot love ourselves as white people, how will we keep showing up? How will we bring our whole embodied selves to the work of racial justice? It is my conviction that we need to love ourselves enough to forge new ways of being white in this world. Imagine if our children and grandchildren could have such role models. What if they could observe us working at unlearning the habits and practices that keep white privilege in place? What if they did not hear us asking, "Is racism really at play in this situation?" and instead heard us asking, "How is racism at play here? And what can we do about it?"

What if our children and grandchildren had white role models who encouraged them to learn about the histories and cultures of BIPOC in their schools, places of worship, and communities? What if they witnessed us listening to, learning from, and quoting people of color in our lives? What if they witnessed us staying in difficult and crucial conversations across race? What if they saw us not shrinking away from the anger of BIPOC, but learning to hold it and honor it? What if they witnessed us feeling and expressing our own anger and grief at racism?

What if our children and grandchildren knew they could turn to us when they were struggling to feel what they are feeling when they see racism and as they search for the courage to speak up and speak out? Imagine if our children and grandchildren had white people in their lives who did not pretend to be color blind, but taught them that it is not difference that divides us but rather the fear of difference and the pathetic pretense that differences do not exist. What if they had the opportunity to experience the gifts of authentic relationships across race and the challenges and joys of multiracial communities?

10. Stay on the Journey

I believe it is possible to claim and embody an antiracist white identity if we are willing to stay on this lifelong journey. Wherever we are on this journey, whether we have been engaged in antiracism activism for years or we are just waking up and wanting to dive deeper, it is never too late for us to bring our hearts, minds, bodies, and resources to the work of interrupting and dismantling racism and white supremacy.

It is never too late to develop new muscles and become agents of change in our spheres of influence. It is never too late to do deep, strenuous, and soul-stretching work so that we can step up with courage, consistency, and cultural humility to participate in the BIPOC-led movements that are working to forge new tipping points. It is never too late to nurture relationships and communities of support and accountability so that we can develop the emotional, physical, and spiritual strength needed to stay the course and become long-distance runners for racial justice.

19

In the Time That I Have Left

We must use what we have to invent what we desire. —ADRIENNE RICH, "To Invent What We Desire," 1993

In 2009, I was asked to speak at a feminist arts event in Lansing, Michigan, called HerStories Fest. Each woman was invited to share, in three minutes' time, what was on her heart and mind, and how she sought to give her feminist passion artistic expression.

I was tempted to share a poem or a story arising from my experience on the margins. As a woman. As a lesbian. As a lesbian feminist woman. I resisted the temptation because I no longer wanted to write and speak as though I only lived at the margins.

In my three-minute presentation, I chose to come out as a lesbian feminist descendant of colonizing English Puritans who landed on the shores of North America in the mid-1600s. I explained that I felt compelled to unearth the stories of my ancestors in order to know from whence I come; to understand more deeply who my people are; to give account of the debts and assets I have inherited as a white woman; and to bring all that I am to the work of naming, resisting, and dismantling the systems that continue to protect white supremacy and patriarchy.

Had I more than three minutes, I might have shared that this passion had intensified exponentially after I turned sixty. Mortality seemed to lurk around every corner, appearing suddenly, sometimes leaving me shaken and grieving. Also sparking in me a fierce urgency.

"In the time that I have left" became my mantra in my sixties. It remains so now that I am in my seventies. It is how I begin my sentences when anyone asks, "What are you up to these days?"

In the time I have left, I want to claim and write in all my voices, those born of privilege as well as those born of oppression. I am not an unraced woman. I am not a lesbian feminist who happens to be white. I cannot embrace Virginia Woolf's declaration: "As a woman I have no country. As a woman I want no country. As a woman my country is the whole world."[1]

In the time that I have left, I want to speak and write in my *white* lesbian feminist voice. Claim it. Risk it. Use it. As a site of embodied feeling and knowing. Not constrained by the fear of saying the wrong thing, yet remaining open to being challenged and corrected. If I ask women of color to share how racism has impacted them, I have to be willing, as a white woman, to share how it has shaped me as a white person. I have to be willing to risk the vulnerability of being fully seen and heard as a white woman. If those of us who are white rely on BIPOC to describe what it means to live in raced bodies, we will become white voyeurs, white spectators, white acquirers of other people's insights and experiences.

In the time that I have left, I want to give attention to the questions that have nagged at me for years, refusing to be silenced or ignored.

In the time that I have left, I want to continue seeking out and learning from the wisdom of BIPOC activists, scholars, poets, novelists, and cultural workers.

In the time that I have left, I want to research and write about my people's history in this country, and work in partnership with others to redress and repair the harm they inflicted.

In the time that I have left, I want to lend my voice and energy to the difficult yet essential work of forging an authentic, accountable, antiracist white identity. I say this knowing that there are dangers and land mines on every hand. The cultural habits of internalized superiority have deep and tenacious roots. We kid ourselves when we think we have excavated them entirely. What we discover along the way must always remain open to critique, evaluation, revision, and continual reinvention. White is not just another color in the multicultural rainbow. White came into existence seizing, controlling, owning, killing, enslaving, codifying, legislating, insisting not only on its difference or distinctness but on its superiority.

In the time that I have left, I want to work in partnership with others to name, confront, and dismantle every contour in the persistent, ever-changing landscape of systemic racism and white supremacy.

In the time that I have left, I hope to never forget that the material benefits and structural power accrued to us as white people are not circumvented or erased by the work of seeking to forge an authentic, accountable antiracist white identity. That work will be of consequence only if it issues in stronger, louder, more creative, and more effective action to dismantle racism and white supremacy.

Acknowledgments

When I contemplate the manifold gifts I have received from mentors, colleagues, and friends, my gratitude is boundless.

I want to acknowledge and thank the antiracism educators who have mentored and inspired me by their courageous truth telling and their indefatigable commitment to a justice rooted in love: Lynnette Stallworth, Donna Bivens, Monique Savage, Shayla Griffin, Dionardo Pizaña, Naomi Ortiz, Nancy Richardson, joan olsson, and Rachel Elizabeth Harding. I am grateful every day for what they have taught me.

It has been an enormous privilege and joy to work with, and learn from, the colleagues with whom I facilitated Doing Our Own Work: An Antiracism Seminar for White People: Eleanor Morrison, Ann Flescher, Aaron Wilson-Ahlstrom, Allyson Bolt, EJ McGaughy Staib, Lois McCullen Parr, Christine Kindy, Dessa Cosma, Autumn Joy Campbell, Diane Schmitz, Jax Lee Gardner, Molly Sweeney, Sara Miller Johnson, Ellis Miller, Hillary Keeney, Joanne Johnson, Michelle McGowen, and Karen Pace. By offering each other love, support, and accountability, we learned how to wrestle with thorny questions, dive deeper still, and embrace complexity, dissonance, and paradox.

With my Allies for Change training partners—Dionardo Pizaña, Monique Savage, Shayla Griffin, Dessa Cosma, Marquita Chamblee, Julia Watts Belser, Rahnee Patrick, and Melinda Haus—I experienced the transformative power of being rooted in a diverse community of colleagues committed to intersectional justice. By rejecting a hierarchy of oppressions and affirming that all of us had much to learn about multiple systems of privilege and oppression, we deepened and expanded our understanding of what it means to be an ally.

During the past five years of ancestral investigations, I have made numerous trips to Montevallo, Alabama, the former home of my enslaving ancestors. I am profoundly grateful to have garnered a new community of mentors, friends, and colleagues who are doing courageous, innovative, and truth-telling work about the history of slavery in Shelby County, Alabama: Kathy King, Carey Heatherly, Joyce Jones, Anitka Sims, Paul Mahaffey, Meredith Tetloff, Jennifer Rickel, Marty Everse, Jennifer Maier, and Peter Datcher. It has been an honor to work collaboratively with these colleagues in the Montevallo Legacy Project, the University of Montevallo Peace and Justice Studies Program, the University of Montevallo Carmichael Library, and the Shelby County Museum and Archives.

I would be remiss if I failed to express my debt to the authors whose conceptual framing, personal stories, and prophetic insights have been foundational for my understanding of white supremacy, systemic racism, the resistance and resilience of BIPOC communities, and what white solidarity looks like: James Baldwin, Toni Morrison, Audre Lorde, Barbara Smith, Claudia Rankine, Joy Harjo, Kimberlé Crenshaw, Aurora Levins Morales, Lillian Smith, Adrienne Rich, Minnie Bruce Pratt, Mab Segrest, and Jennifer Harvey.

It has been a great joy to once again work with Duke University Press. I am especially indebted to my editor, Gisela Concepción Fosado, who recognized the possibilities of this book while it was still taking shape. Her discerning vision, wise feedback, and enthusiastic support helped bring this project to completion. I also want to thank her editorial associate, Alejandra Mejia, who responded to every inquiry with patience and expertise. The incisive insights and suggested revisions I received from the peer reviewers helped make this a better book.

To my beloved spouse, April Allison: You were there, from the moment this project first took hold of me, through late nights when I insisted on reading the latest revisions aloud to you, to the day I felt it was finished, and you nodded your approval. With pen in hand, you offered exceptional editorial feedback every step of the way. And your love, as always, kept me grounded and able to carry on.

Notes

CHAPTER 1. BECOMING TRUSTWORTHY WHITE ALLIES

"Becoming Trustworthy White Allies" was originally published in *Reflections* (Spring 2013): 73–75.

1. Terry, "Negative Impact on White Values," 120.
2. This exercise is adapted from an activity created and led by Frances Kendall and Paul Kivel at the 2003 National Conference on Race and Ethnicity.
3. McIntosh, "White Privilege and Male Privilege," 9.
4. I am indebted to Kate Runyon for this image.
5. For a helpful list of questions to identify and assess cultures of power within organizations, see Kivel, "Culture of Power," 52–56.
6. See Pizaña, "Authenticity in a Community Setting." Pizaña describes how outreach programs are too often grounded in a savior mentality that fails to honor the wisdom and culture of the people being served. He suggests an alternative model known as "in-reach" programs that seek to incorporate and build upon the wisdom, assets, and leadership of all parties involved.
7. Lorde, "Uses of Anger," 130.
8. I am indebted to Ruth Frankenberg for her insight that antiracist work by white people requires "doing the work from a place of self-love." Frankenberg's journey as an antiracist activist and writer is described by Becky Thompson in *Promise and a Way of Life*, 162–66.
9. Rose, "White Identity and Counseling," 42.

CHAPTER 5. WHY AN ANTIRACISM SEMINAR FOR WHITE PEOPLE

1. Kaufman, *Shame*, 8.

CHAPTER 8. CULTURAL ENVY

1 Nobles, "Infusion of African and African-American Content," 1.
2 See McIntosh, "White Privilege."
3 See Baldwin, "Price of the Ticket," xix.

CHAPTER 9. GENEALOGY AS SPIRITUAL PRACTICE

"Genealogy as Spiritual Practice: Reflections on My White Ancestral Work" was previously published in *Geez*, no. 70 (Fall 2023): 24–27.

1 Morales, "Raícism," 99.

CHAPTER 10. WHY WE MUST REMEMBER

1 Johnson, *Lives and Times of Kingswood*.
2 Johnson, *Lives and Times of Kingswood*, 4–7; Meroney, *Montevallo*, 8–11; Nutting, "Montevallo," 20–22; Clifton, "Montevallo in 1886"; "How King Came to Be."
3 About William Weatherford, see Jones, "William Weatherford and the Road"; Griffith, *McIntosh and Weatherford*; and Saunt, *New Order of Things*.
4 For Montevallo ghost stories, see Kocsis, "Campus Ghost Stories"; Love, "Local Haunts"; and Windham, "Ghosts at Montevallo's Mansion House."
5 *Murder on Shades Mountain: The Legal Lynching of Willie Peterson and the Struggle for Justice in Jim Crow Birmingham* was published by Duke University Press in 2018. Framed by memoir, *Murder on Shades Mountain* is a historical narrative about events that shook the city of Birmingham, Alabama, in the early 1930s when three white women were brutally attacked, and a Black man named Willie Peterson was unjustly convicted and sentenced to die.
6 For sources about the meaning of ghosts in African American cultural traditions, see Gordon, *Ghostly Matters*, 137–90; Harding with Harding, "Hospitality, Haints, and Healing," 98–114; Krumholz, "Ghosts of History," 395–408; Miles, *Tales from the Haunted South*, 115–32; Stewart, *Long Past Slavery*, 1–3; and Wells-Oghoghomeh, *Souls of Womenfolk*, 147–48, 170–72, 185–86.
7 Morrison, "On *Beloved*," 284.
8 Montagne, "Toni Morrison's 'Good' Ghosts."
9 "Mrs. Elizabeth King Shortridge."
10 "Pioneer Resident Passed Away June 30."
11 See Clifton, "Montevallo in 1886"; Johnson, *Lives and Times of Kingswood*; Meroney, *Montevallo*.
12 Everse, "King Had a Hammer," 3; Meroney, *Montevallo*, 10–11.
13 For the history of the Creek War, Andrew Jackson's military campaigns, and the forced dispossession of the Muscogee people, see Black, "Memories of the Alabama Creek War"; Kanon, "Before Horseshoe"; and Waselkov, "Fort Jackson and the Aftermath."
14 Bureau of Land Management, "Land Patent Search," digital images, General Land Office Records, https://glorecords.blm.gov/search/default.aspx.

15 Bureau of Land Management, "Land Patent Search."
16 Saunt, *Unworthy Republic*, 245.
17 1830 United States Federal Census: Census Place: Shelby, Alabama; Series: M19; Roll: 2; Page: 262; Family History Library Film: 0002329, http://www.ancestry.com.
18 Deyle, "'Abominable New Trade,'" 841; see also Berry, *Price for Their Pound of Flesh*, 1–9.
19 See Martin, "Slavery's Invisible Engine."
20 Will Record H 1856–1867, 857–83, Shelby County Museum and Archives, Columbiana, Alabama.
21 Will Record H, 872.
22 For impact on enslaved people, see Williams, *Help Me to Find My People*, 21–25.
23 For sources on the rupture of enslaved families, see Baptist, *Half Has Never Been Told*, 106–7; Field, "Violence of Family Formation"; and Williams, *Help Me to Find My People*.
24 Camp, *Closer to Freedom*, 59–92. For information about the resistance of enslaved women, see Camp, "Pleasures of Resistance," 533–72.
25 See Harjo, *American Sunrise*. For an interview with Joy Harjo, see Chiabattari, "Joy Harjo."
26 For information about Universities Studying Slavery, see University of Virginia, President's Commission on Slavery and the University, https://slavery.virginia.edu/universities-studying-slavery/.
27 Hannah-Jones, "Preface," in Hannah-Jones et al., *1619 Project*, xxiii.
28 The Montevallo Legacy Project, a community action organization founded in 2022, is dedicated to giving voice and visibility to the untold stories of Montevallo's African American community: https://themontevallolegacyproject.com.

CHAPTER 11. A JUST RECKONING

1 Smith, *How the Word Is Passed*, 289.
2 Johnson, *Lives and Times of Kingswood*, ix, 17, 23, 93, 96.
3 Everse, "King Had a Hammer"; "Early Days in and Around Montevallo"; and Meroney, *Montevallo*, 8–11.
4 Johnson, *Lives and Times of Kingswood*, 3, 6, 30, 49, 51.
5 1830 United States Federal Census: Census Place: Shelby, Alabama; Series: M19; Roll: 2; Page: 262; Family History Library Film: 0002329, http://www.ancestry.com.
6 Johnson, *Lives and Times of Kingswood*, 31.
7 For the history of the Creek War, Andrew Jackson's military campaigns, and the forced dispossession of the Muscogee people, see Black, "Memories of the Alabama Creek War"; Davis, "'Remember Fort Mims'"; Haveman, *Bending Their Way Onward*; Haveman, *Rivers of Sand*; Inskeep, *Jacksonland*; Kanon, "Before Horseshoe"; Perdue, "Legacy of Indian Removal"; and Waselkov, "Fort Jackson and the Aftermath."
8 Meroney, *Montevallo*, 5.
9 Meroney, *Montevallo*, 5–6.

10 For information about William Rufus King's landholdings in Alabama, see Balcerski, *Bosom Friends*, 43–45; and Brooks, "Faces of William Rufus King," 14–23.
11 Bureau of Land Management, "Land Patent Search," digital images, General Land Office Records, https://glorecords.blm.gov/search/default.aspx.
12 Bureau of Land Management, "Land Patent Search."
13 "Negroes and Cotton."
14 Glymph, *Out of the House of Bondage*, 28.
15 Glymph, *Out of the House of Bondage*, 20.
16 Jones-Rogers, *They Were Her Property*, xii.
17 Jones-Rogers, *They Were Her Property*, xiv.
18 Johnson, *Lives and Times of Kingswood*, 35.
19 For information about George D. Shortridge's financial problems, see Roberts, "Banking Hiatus of George D. Shortridge," 172–87.
20 Roberts, "Banking Hiatus of George D. Shortridge," 185–86.
21 Deed Book N, 892–93, Shelby County Museum and Archives, Columbiana, Alabama.
22 Deed Book 1842–1847, Book 801-2, 206, Shelby County Museum and Archives.
23 Burnham, "Impossible Marriage," 189.
24 Burnham, "Impossible Marriage," 199.
25 Jones-Rogers, *They Were Her Property*, xx.
26 Camp, *Closer to Freedom*, 2–3.
27 Camp, *Closer to Freedom*, 61–63.
28 1860 United State Federal Census—Slave Schedules, Edmund King, Shelby County, June 1, 1860, http://www.ancestry.com.
29 Camp, *Closer to Freedom*, 36.
30 Camp, *Closer to Freedom*, 47–53.
31 Camp, *Closer to Freedom*, 7.
32 Deed Book L, 164–65, Shelby County Museum and Archives.
33 For the social value of enslaved midwives, see Goode and Rothman, "African-American Midwifery," 72–74.
34 Loose court record of the Third District of the Shelby County Circuit Court, June 1859, Shelby County Museum and Archives.
35 Deed Book L, 165, Shelby County Museum and Archives.
36 Deed Book M, 1857–1859, 802-1, 355, Shelby County Museum and Archives.
37 Deed Book N, 109, Shelby County Museum and Archives.
38 Miles, *All That She Carried*, xiv.
39 Hannah-Jones, "Preface," in Hannah-Jones et al., *1619 Project*, xxiii.

CHAPTER 13. SOUL SPLITTING

1 Blackmon, *Slavery by Another Name*, 106.
2 Goldsby, *A Spectacular Secret*, 65.
3 Ifill, *On the Courthouse Lawn*, xii.
4 Ifill, *On the Courthouse Lawn*, xiii.

5 Ifill, *On the Courthouse Lawn*, xi.
6 Apel, *Imagery of Lynching*, 41.
7 Apel, "Lynching Photographs and the Politics," 56.
8 Ifill, *On the Courthouse Lawn*, 133.

CHAPTER 15. TRAYVON MARTIN, THE LEGACY OF LYNCHING, AND THE ROLE OF WHITE WOMEN

"Trayvon Martin, the Legacy of Lynching, and the Role of White Women" was originally published online in the author's blog on July 13, 2018, the fifth anniversary of the exoneration of George Zimmerman; see https://www.melaniemorrison.net/blog/trayvon-martin-the-legacy-of-lynching-and-the-role-of-white-women.

1 Among the books Lillian Smith wrote, I would especially recommend *Killers of the Dream* (1949), *Now Is the Time* (1955), and *The Winner Names the Age: A Collection of Writings* (1978).
2 For analyses of lynching, see Jordan, "Crossing the River of Blood"; Clegg, *A Troubled Ground*; Ifill, *On the Courthouse Lawn*; Wood, *Lynching and Spectacle*; and Feimster, *Southern Horrors*.
3 Jordan, "Crossing the River of Blood," 554.
4 In Wells-Barnett, "Miss Willard's Attitude," Wells takes Frances Willard, leader of the Women's Christian Temperance Union, to task for her silence and culpability in failing to condemn lynching; see also hooks, *Talking Back*; the work of Ruby Sales, founder and director of Breaking the Silence Against Modern Day Lynching, a program of the SpiritHouse Project (https://www.spirithouseproject.org), that documents and records issues, articles, and photographs on the rising rate of modern lynchings, beatings, and drownings (torture) by white police and vigilantes; and Jordan, "Crossing the River of Blood."
5 Jordan, "Crossing the River of Blood," 556.
6 Florida, "It's Not Just Zimmerman."
7 For an in-depth analysis of Judge Nolan's rulings and instructions to the jury, see Cone, "Unbelievable Directions and Instructions."
8 See the video of the press conference called by Angela Corey and her prosecution team in "Angela Corey, Prosecutors Speak."
9 Blow, "Whole System Failed."
10 Matthews, "Here's What You Need to Know."
11 Hill, "Trayvon Martin Was Put on Trial."
12 Transcript of Cooper, "Exclusive Interview with Juror B-37."
13 See "Angela Corey, Prosecutors Speak."
14 Jordan, "Crossing the River of Blood," 580.

CHAPTER 16. AT THE HANDS OF PERSONS UNKNOWN

"At the Hands of Persons Unknown" was originally posted in the author's blog on May 26, 2015; see https://www.melaniemorrison.net/blog/at-the-hand-of-persons-unknown.

1. Hanna et al., "Cleveland Officer Not Guilty."
2. See Equal Justice Initiative, *Lynching in America*.
3. See Dray, *At the Hands of Persons Unknown*.
4. Hanna et al., "Cleveland Officer Not Guilty."
5. Lieszkovszky, "Why the Judge Found."
6. Lieszkovszky, "Why the Judge Found."
7. Neuman, "Cleveland Officer Acquitted."

CHAPTER 17. "THE FIERCE URGENCY OF NOW"

"The Fierce Urgency of Now" was originally published online in *Radical Discipleship* on April 1, 2017; see https://radicaldiscipleship.net/2017/04/01/the-fierce-urgency-of-now/.

1. For a complete text and an audio recording of Dr. King's speech, see King, "Beyond Vietnam."
2. Coates, *Between the World and Me*, 103.
3. Bouie, "Michael Brown Wasn't a Superhuman Demon."
4. Hassan, "Sandra Bland Video."

CHAPTER 18. WHAT WILL IT TAKE FOR WHITE PEOPLE TO STAY THE COURSE?

1. Buchanan et al., "Black Lives Matter."
2. Bose and Thompson, "White Americans Turn Out."
3. Harmon and Tavernise, "One Big Difference."
4. See Terry Gross's interview with Jeffrey Sachs, Gross, "From Slavery to Socialism."
5. Taylor, "Did Last Summer's Black Lives Matter Protests."
6. Taylor, "Did Last Summer's Black Lives Matter Protests."
7. McIntosh, "White Privilege and Male Privilege," 9.
8. Morales, "Raícism," 103.
9. Browning, "Crime Against Humanity."
10. Kendall, *Understanding White Privilege*, 62.
11. Rose, "White Identity and Counseling," 42.
12. Bivens and Richardson, "Naming and Claiming Our Histories," 12.
13. Standley and Pratt, *Conversations with James Baldwin*, 156.
14. For an excellent guide to the principles of antiracist accountability, see Cushing et al., *Accountability and White Anti-Racist Organizing*.
15. Walker, *Her Blue Body*, 155.
16. Baldwin, *Fire Next Time*, 109.

17 I am indebted to Ruth Frankenberg for her insight that antiracist work by white people requires "doing the work from a place of self-love." Frankenberg's journey as an antiracist activist and writer is described in Thompson, *Promise and a Way of Life*, 162–66. For reflections of antiracism, love, and compassionate self-awareness, also see Okun, *Emperor Has No Clothes*, xxvii–xxx.

CHAPTER 19. IN THE TIME THAT I HAVE LEFT

1 Woolf, *Three Guineas*, 94.

Bibliography

Allen, James. *Without Sanctuary: Lynching Photography in America.* Santa Fe, NM: Twin Palms Publisher, 1999.
"Angela Corey, Prosecutors Speak About George Zimmerman Not Guilty Verdict." WESH 2, July 13, 2013. https://www.wesh.com/article/angela-corey-prosecutors-speak-about-george-zimmerman-not-guilty-verdict/3796315#!bbRnxh.
Apel, Dora. *Imagery of Lynching: Black Men, White Women, and the Mob.* New Brunswick, NJ: Rutgers University Press, 2004.
Apel, Dora. "Lynching Photographs and the Politics of Public Shaming." In *Lynching Photographs*, vol. 2, by Dora Apel and Shawn Michelle Smith. Oakland: University of California Press, 2008.
Balcerski, Thomas J. *Bosom Friends: The Intimate World of James Buchanan and William Rufus King.* New York: Oxford University Press, 2019.
Baldwin, James. *The Fire Next Time.* New York: Dial, 1963.
Baldwin, James. "The Price of the Ticket." In *The Price of the Ticket: Collected Nonfiction, 1948-1985.* New York: St. Martin's, 1985.
Baptist, Edward E. *The Half Has Never Been Told: Slavery and the Making of American Capitalism.* New York: Basic Books, 2014.
Berry, Daina Ramey. *The Price for Their Pound of Flesh: The Value of the Enslaved, from Womb to Grave, in the Building of a Nation.* Boston: Beacon, 2017.
Bivens, Donna K., and Nancy D. Richardson. "Naming and Claiming Our Histories." *Brown Papers* 1, no. 2 (November 1994).
Black, Jason Edward. "Memories of the Alabama Creek War, 1813-1814: U.S. Governmental and Native Identities at the Horseshoe Bend National Military Park." *American Indian Quarterly* 33, no. 2 (Spring 2009): 200-229.
Blackmon, Douglas A. *Slavery by Another Name: The Re-Enslavement of Black Americans from the Civil War to World War II.* New York: Doubleday, 2018.
Blow, Charles. "The Whole System Failed Trayvon Martin." *New York Times*, July 15, 2013.
Bose, Nandita, and Heather Thompson. "White Americans Turn Out for Floyd Protests, but Will They Work for Change?" *Reuters*, June 11, 2020.

Bouie, Jamelle. "Michael Brown Wasn't a Superhuman Demon." *Slate*, November 26, 2014. https://slate.com/news-and-politics/2014/11/darren-wilsons-racial-portrayal-of-michael-brown-as-a-superhuman-demon-the-ferguson-police-officers-account-is-a-common-projection-of-racial-fears.html.

Braund, Kathryn E. Holland, ed. *Tohopeka: Remembering the Creek War and the War of 1812.* Tuscaloosa: University of Alabama Press, 2012.

Brooks, Daniel Fate. "The Faces of William Rufus King." *Alabama Heritage* 69 (Summer 2003): 14–23.

Browning, Sarah. "A Crime Against Humanity Sent Me to Harvard." *Other Words*, June 24, 2015. https://otherwords.org/a-crime-against-humanity-sent-me-to-harvard/.

Buchanan, Larry, Bui Quoctrung, and Jugal K. Patel. "Black Lives Matter May Be the Largest Movement in U.S. History." *New York Times*, July 3, 2020.

Bulkin, Elly, Minnie Bruce Pratt, and Barbara Smith. *Yours in the Struggle: Three Feminist Perspectives on Anti-Semitism and Racism.* New York: Long Haul Press, 1984.

Burnham, Margaret A. "An Impossible Marriage: Slave Law and Family Law." *Minnesota Journal of Law and Inequality* 5, no. 2 (1987): 187–225.

Camp, Stephanie M. H. *Closer to Freedom: Enslaved Women and Everyday Resistance in the Plantation South.* Chapel Hill: University of North Carolina Press, 2004.

Camp, Stephanie M. H. "The Pleasures of Resistance: Enslaved Women and Body Politics in the Plantation South, 1830–1861." *Journal of Southern History* 68, no. 3 (2002): 533–72.

Chiabattari, Jane. "Joy Harjo: A Preview." *Pen America*, April 22, 2013. https://pen.org/joy-harjo-a-preview/.

Clegg, Claude A. *A Troubled Ground: A Tale of Murder, Lynching, and Reckoning in the New South.* Champaign: University of Illinois Press, 2010.

Clifton, Clyde. "Montevallo in 1886." *Shelby County Times-Herald*, February 19, 1959. Reprinted from *Birmingham Sunday Chronicle*, December 19, 1886.

Coates, Ta-Nehisi. *Between the World and Me.* New York: Spiegel and Grau, 2015.

Cone, Marjorie. "Unbelievable Directions and Instructions from Judge Sway Jury in Zimmerman Trial." *San Diego Free Press*, July 18, 2013.

Cooper, Anderson. "Exclusive Interview with Juror B-37." *360 Degrees*, July 15, 2013. https://transcripts.cnn.com/show/acd/date/2013-07-15/segment/01.

Cushing, Bonnie Berman, with Lila Cabbil, Margery Freeman, Jeff Hitchcock, and Kimberley Richards. *Accountability and White Anti-Racist Organizing: Stories from Our Work.* Harrisburg, PA: Crandall, Dostie and Douglass, 2010.

Davis, Karl Arthur. "'Remember Fort Mims': Reinterpreting the Origins of the Creek War." *Journal of the Early Republic* 22, no. 4 (Winter 2002).

Deyle, Steven. "An 'Abominable' New Trade: The Closing of the African Slave Trade and the Changing Patterns of U.S. Political Power, 1808–60." *William and Mary Quarterly* 66, no. 4 (2009): 833–50.

Dray, Philip. *At the Hands of Persons Unknown: The Lynching of Black America.* New York: Random House, 2002.

"Early Days in and Around Montevallo." *Montevallo News*, September 5, 1895.

Equal Justice Initiative. *Lynching in America: Confronting the Legacy of Racial Terror.* 3rd ed. 2017.

Everse, Marty. "King Had a Hammer." *Chamber Chatter* 17, no. 7 (July 2019).

Feimster, Crystal M. *Southern Horrors: Women and the Politics of Rape and Lynching.* Cambridge, MA: Harvard University Press, 2011.

Field, Kendra. "The Violence of Family Formation: Enslaved Families and Reproductive Labor in the Marketplace." *Reviews in American History* 42, no. 2 (2014): 255–64.

Florida, Richard. "It's Not Just Zimmerman: Race Matters a Lot in 'Stand Your Ground Verdicts.'" *Atlantic City Lab,* July 16, 2013.

Frankenberg, Ruth. *White Women, Race Matters: The Social Construction of Whiteness.* Minneapolis: University of Minnesota Press, 1993.

Glymph, Thavolia. *Out of the House of Bondage: The Transformation of the Plantation Household.* New York: Cambridge University Press, 2008.

Goldsby, Jacqueline. *A Spectacular Secret: Lynching in American Life and Literature.* Chicago: University of Chicago Press, 2006.

Goode, Keisha, and Barbara Katz Rothman. "African-American Midwifery, a History and a Lament." *American Journal of Economics and Sociology* 76, no. 1 (2017): 65–94. http://www.jstor.org/stable/45129363.

Gordon, Avery F. *Ghostly Matters: Haunting and the Sociological Imagination.* New ed. Minneapolis: University of Minnesota Press, 2008.

Griffin, Shayla Reese. "Where 'Diversity Training' Goes Wrong." *Medium,* February 6, 2021. https://medium.com/@shaylargriffin/where-diversity-training-goes-wrong-10-essential-questions-to-ask-1217863eab04.

Griffith, Benjamin, Jr. *McIntosh and Weatherford, Creek Indian Leaders.* Tuscaloosa: University of Alabama Press, 1998.

Gross, Terry. "From Slavery to Socialism, New Legislation Restricts What Teachers Can Discuss." *Fresh Air,* NPR, February 3, 2020. https://www.npr.org/2022/02/03/1077878538/legislation-restricts-what-teachers-can-discuss.

Hanna, Jason, Ralph Ellis, and Greg Botelho. "Cleveland Officer Not Guilty in Killing Unarmed Pair." CNN, May 23, 2015. https://www.cnn.com/2015/05/23/us/cleveland-police-verdict/.

Hannah-Jones, Nikole, Caitlin Roper, Ilena Silverman, and Jake Silverstein, eds. *The 1619 Project, A New Origin Story.* New York: New York Times Company, 2019.

Harding, Rosemarie Freeney, with Rachel Elizabeth Harding. "Hospitality, Haints, and Healing: A Southern African Meaning of Religion." In *Deeper Shades of Purple: Womanism in Religion and Society,* edited by Stacey M. Floyd-Thomas. New York: New York University Press, 2006.

Harding, Rosemarie Freeney, with Rachel Elizabeth Harding. *Remnants: A Memoir of Spirit, Activism, and Mothering.* Durham, NC: Duke University Press, 2015.

Harjo, Joy. *An American Sunrise, Poems.* New York: W. W. Norton, 2019.

Harmon, Amy, and Sabrina Tavernise. "One Big Difference About George Floyd Protests: Many White Faces." *New York Times,* June 17, 2020.

Harvey, Jennifer. *Raising White Kids: Bringing Up Children in a Racially Unjust America.* Nashville, TN: Abingdon Press, 2018.

Hassan, Adeel. "The Sandra Bland Video: What We Know." *New York Times,* May 7, 2019. https://www.nytimes.com/2019/05/07/us/sandra-bland-brian-encinia.html.

Haveman, Christopher D. *Bending Their Way Onward: Creek Indian Removal in Documents*. Lincoln: University of Nebraska Press, 2018.

Haveman, Christopher D. *Rivers of Sand: Creek Indian Emigration, Relocation, and Ethnic Cleansing in the American South*. Lincoln: University of Nebraska Press, 2016.

Hill, Marc Lamont. "Trayvon Martin Was Put on Trial." *Black Enterprise Blogs*, July 9, 2013.

hooks, bell. *Talking Back: Thinking Black, Thinking Feminist*. Boston: South End Press, 1989.

"How King Came to Be." Anna Crawford Milner Archives and Special Collections, Carmichael Library, University of Montevallo. Last updated June 11, 2024. https://libguides.montevallo.edu/archives/KingHouse.

Ifill, Sherrilyn A. *On the Courthouse Lawn: Confronting the Legacy of Lynching in the Twenty-First Century*. Boston: Beacon, 2007.

Inskeep, Steve. *Jacksonland: President Andrew Jackson, Cherokee Chief John Ross, and a Great American Land Grab*. New York: Penguin, 2016.

Johnson, Golda W. *The Lives and Times of Kingswood in Alabama, 1817–1890*. Montevallo, AL: University of Montevallo, 1976.

Jones, Pam. "William Weatherford and the Road to the Holy Ground." *Alabama Heritage* 74 (Fall 2004): 24–32.

Jones-Rogers, Stephanie. *They Were Her Property: White Women as Slave Owners in the American South*. New Haven, CT: Yale University Press, 2019.

Jordan, Emma Coleman. "Crossing the River of Blood Between Us: Lynching, Violence, Beauty, and the Paradox of Feminist History." *Journal of Gender, Race and Justice* 3 (2000): 545–80. http://scholarship.law.georgetown.edu/facpub/101.

Kanon, Tom. "Before Horseshoe: Andrew Jackson's Campaigns in the Creek War Prior to Horseshoe Bend." In *Tohopeka: Rethinking the Creek War and the War of 1812*. Tuscaloosa: University of Alabama Press, 2012.

Kaufman, Gershen. *Shame: The Power of Caring*. Rochester, VT: Shenkman, 1980.

Kendall, Frances. *Understanding White Privilege: Creating Pathways to Authentic Relationships Across Race*. New York: Routledge, 2006.

King, Martin Luther, Jr. "Beyond Vietnam: A Time to Break Silence." *American Rhetoric*, October 3, 2010. https://www.americanrhetoric.com/speeches/mlkatimetobreaksilence.htm.

Kivel, Paul. "The Culture of Power." *Uprooting Racism: How White People Can Work for Racial Justice*. Gabriola Island, BC: New Society, 2002.

Kocsis, Annaprenzie. "Campus Ghost Stories." *Alabamian*, October 18, 2020. https://www.thealabamian.com/campus-ghost-stories/.

Krumholz, Linda. "The Ghosts of History: Historical Recovery in Toni Morrison's *Beloved*." *African American Review* 26, no. 3 (Autumn 1992): 395–408.

Lieszkovszky, Ida. "Why the Judge Found Cleveland Police Officer Michael Brelo Not Guilty." *Cleveland.com*, May 23, 2015. https://www.cleveland.com/court-justice/2015/05/why_the_judge_found_cleveland.html.

Lorde, Audre. "Age, Race, Class, and Sex: Women Redefining Difference." In *Sister Outsider: Essays and Speeches*. Trumansburg, NY: Crossing Press, 1984.

Lorde, Audre. "The Uses of Anger: Women Responding to Racism." In *Sister Outsider: Essays and Speeches*. Trumansburg, NY: Crossing Press, 1984.

Love, Michelle. "Local Haunts: The Chilling History of Shelby County." *Shelby County Reporter*, November 3, 2021. https://www.shelbycountyreporter.com/2021/11/03/local-haunts-the-chilling-history-of-shelby-county/.

Martin, Bonnie. "Slavery's Invisible Engine: Mortgaging Human Property." *Journal of Southern History* 76, no. 4 (2010): 817–66.

Matthews, Dylan. "Here's What You Need to Know About Stop and Frisk—and Why the Courts Shut It Down." *Washington Post*, August 13, 2013.

McIntosh, Peggy. "White Privilege and Male Privilege: A Personal Account of Coming to See Correspondences Through Work in Women's Studies." Working Paper No. 189, Center for Research on Women. Wellesley, MA: Wellesley College, 1988.

McIntosh, Peggy. "White Privilege: Unpacking the Invisible Knapsack." *Peace and Freedom Magazine*, July/August 1989, 10–12.

Meroney, Eloise. *Montevallo: The First One Hundred Years*. Montevallo: Times Printing, 1977. http://www.historicmontevallo.org/ewExternalFiles/Montevallo%20Meroney.pdf.

Miles, Tiya. *All That She Carried: The Journey of Ashley's Sack, a Black Family Keepsake*. New York: Random House, 2021.

Miles, Tiya. *Tales from the Haunted South: Dark Tourism and Memories of Slavery from the Civil War Era*. Chapel Hill: University of North Carolina Press, 2016.

Montagne, Renee. "Toni Morrison's 'Good' Ghosts." *Morning Edition*, NPR News, September 20, 2004. https://www.npr.org/transcripts/3912464.

Morales, Aurora Levins. "Raícism: Rootedness and Spiritual and Political Practice." In *Medicine Stories: Essays for Radicals*. Rev. and expanded ed. Durham, NC: Duke University Press, 2019.

Morrison, Melanie S. *Murder on Shades Mountain: The Legal Lynching of Willie Peterson and the Struggle for Justice in Jim Crow Birmingham*. Durham, NC: Duke University Press, 2018.

Morrison, Toni. *Beloved*. New York: Vintage, 2004.

Morrison, Toni. "On *Beloved*." In *The Source of Self-Regard: Selected Essays, Speeches, and Meditations*. New York: Alfred A. Knopf, 2018.

Morrison, Toni. "Unspeakable Things Unspoken: The Afro-American Presence in American Literature." In *The Source of Self-Regard: Selected Essays, Speeches, and Meditations*. New York: Alfred A. Knopf, 2018.

"Mrs. Elizabeth King Shortridge." *Austin American-Statesman*, January 14, 1906.

"Negroes and Cotton, Factory for Sale." *Independent Monitor*, November 12, 1857.

Neuman, Scott. "Cleveland Officer Acquitted in 2012 Fatal Shooting of Unarmed Suspects." *The Two-Way*, NPR, May 23, 2015. https://www.npr.org/sections/thetwo-way/2015/05/23/409003419/cleveland-officer-not-guilty-in-fatal-shooting-of-unarmed-suspects.

Nobles, Wade W. "The Infusion of African and African-American Content: A Question of Content and Intent." National Urban Alliance for Effective Education, n.d. https://www.nuatc.org/articles/pdf/Nobles_article.pdf.

Nutting, Alissa. "Montevallo, Mound in a Valley." *Alabama Heritage*, Spring 2007, 18–29.

Okun, Tema. *The Emperor Has No Clothes: Teaching About Race and Racism to People Who Don't Want to Know*. Charlotte, NC: Information Age, 2010.

olsson, joan. *Detour-Spotting for White Anti-Racists*. Pamphlet. Questa, NM: Cultural Bridges, January 1997, 2005, 2011.

Perdue, Theda. "The Legacy of Indian Removal." *Journal of Southern History* 78, no. 1 (2012): 3–36.

"Pioneer Resident Passed Away June 30." *Shelby County Reporter*, July 9, 1942.

Pizaña, Dionardo. "Authenticity in a Community Setting—a Tool for Self-Reflection and Change." Diversity, Equity and Inclusion: Community of Practice, 2003. https://copdei.extension.org/authenticity-in-a-community-setting-a-tool-for-self-reflection-and-change/.

Rankine, Claudia. *Citizen: An American Lyric*. Minneapolis: Grey Wolf Press, 2014.

Rich, Adrienne. *Blood, Bread, and Poetry*. New York: W. W. Norton, 1986.

Rich, Adrienne. "To Invent What We Desire." In *What Is Found There: Notes on Poetry and Politics*. New York: W. W. Norton, 1993.

Roberts, Barbara. "The Banking Hiatus of George D. Shortridge." *Alabama Review* 32, no. 3 (July 1979): 172–87.

Rose, Lillian Roybal. "White Identity and Counseling White Allies About Racism." In *Impacts of Racism on White Americans*, 2nd ed., edited by Benjamin P. Bowser and Raymond G. Hunt. Thousand Oaks, CA: Sage, 1996.

Saunt, Claudio. *A New Order of Things: Property, Power, and the Transformation of the Creek Indians, 1733–1816*. Cambridge: Cambridge University Press, 1999.

Saunt, Claudio. *Unworthy Republic: The Dispossession of Native Americans and the Road to Indian Territory*. Illustrated ed. New York: W. W. Norton, 2020.

Segrest, Mab. *Born to Belonging: Writings on Spirit and Justice*. New Brunswick, NJ: Rutgers University Press, 2002.

Segrest, Mab. *Memoir of a Race Traitor*. Reprint ed. New York: New Press, 2019.

Smith, Clint. *How the Word Is Passed: A Reckoning with the History of Slavery Across America*. Boston, MA: Little, Brown, 2021.

Smith, Lillian. *Killers of the Dream*. New York: W. W. Norton, 1994.

Smith, Lillian. *Now Is the Time: Segregation, the Supreme Court, and Democracy*. New York: Viking, 1955.

Smith, Lillian. *The Winner Names the Age: A Collection of Writings*. New York: W. W. Norton, 1978.

Standley, Fred L., and Louis H. Pratt. *Conversations with James Baldwin*. Literary Conversations Series. Jackson: University Press of Mississippi, 1989.

Stewart, Catherine A. *Long Past Slavery: Representing Race in the Federal Writer's Project*. Chapel Hill: University of North Carolina Press, 2016.

Taylor, Keeanga-Yamahtta. "Did Last Summer's Black Lives Matter Protests Change Anything?" *New Yorker*, August 6, 2021. https://www.newyorker.com/news/our-columnists/did-last-summers-protests-change-anything.

Terry, Robert W. "The Negative Impact on White Values." In *Impacts of Racism on White Americans*, edited by Benjamin P. Bowser and Raymond G. Hunt. Thousand Oaks, CA: Sage, 1981.

Thompson, Becky. *A Promise and a Way of Life: White Antiracist Activism*. Minneapolis: University of Minnesota, 2001.

Tochluk, Shelly, and Cameron Levin. "Powerful Partnerships: Transformative Alliance Building." In *Accountability and White Anti-Racist Organizing: Stories from Our Work*. Harrisburg, PA: Crandall, Dostie and Douglass, 2010.

Walker, Alice. *Anything We Love Can Be Saved: A Writer's Activism*. New York: Ballantine, 1998.

Walker, Alice. *Her Blue Body Everything We Know: Earthling Poems 1965-1990 Complete*. Boston: Mariner, 2003.

Waselkov, Gregory A. "Fort Jackson and the Aftermath." In *Tohopeka: Rethinking the Creek War and the War of 1812*. Tuscaloosa: University of Alabama Press, 2012.

Wells-Barnett, Ida B. "Miss Willard's Attitude." In *On Lynchings*. Mineola, NY: Dover, 2014.

Wells-Oghoghomeh, Alexis. *The Souls of Womenfolk: The Religious Cultures of Enslaved Women in the Lower South*. Chapel Hill: University of North Carolina Press, 2021.

Williams, Heather Andrea. *Help Me to Find My People: The African American Search for Family Lost in Slavery*. Chapel Hill: University of North Carolina Press, 2012.

Windham, Kathryn Tucker. "The Ghosts at Montevallo's Mansion House." In *Jeffrey's Latest Thirteen: More Alabama Ghosts*. Commemorative ed. Tuscaloosa: University of Alabama Press, 2016.

Wise, Tim. "Appreciation and Accountability." Accessed April 4, 2017. (Document no longer retrievable.)

Wood, Amy Louise. *Lynching and Spectacle: Witnessing Racial Violence in America, 1890-1940*. Chapel Hill: University of North Carolina Press, 2011.

Woolf, Virginia. *Three Guineas: The Virginia Woolf Library Authorized Edition*. Boston: Mariner Books, Houghton Mifflin Harcourt, 1938.

Index

accountable relationships, 6, 16, 36, 37, 42–45
Allies for Change, 6–7, 8
Allison, April, 27–29, 71, 110
Ally Training Partners, 6
Amanda (enslaved person), 81–82
Ann (Anny, enslaved person), 85–86
antiracist allies, 25–26, 133–47, 149–51; definition of, 25
Association of Southern Women for the Prevention of Lynching (ASWPL), 114

Baldwin, James, 55, 142, 145–46
Battle of Horseshoe Bend, 77
Birmingham (AL), 59, 101–12
Birmingham Public Library Archives, 108, 110
Birmingham-Southern College, 107
Bivens, Donna, 2, 3, 9
Bland, Sandra, 129
Blocton, Alabama, 96
Blow, Charles, 116
book bans, 135
Brelo, Michael, 123–25
Briscoe Center for American History, 88
Brown, Michael, 129
Browning, Sarah, 137
Burnham, Margaret, 81

Cahaba Valley (AL), 77, 78
Camp, Stephanie, 72, 82–83
Carmichael Library, 86
Caroline (enslaved person), 82

Charleston Church massacre, 47
Chief Red Eagle, 63. *See also* Weatherford, William
Cleveland (OH), 123–25
Coates, Ta-Nehisi, 128
communities of resistance, 138, 143–44
convict lease system, 59–60
Cooper, Anderson, 117–18
Corey, Angela, 115, 116, 118–19
cotton mill (Bibb County, AL), 76, 78
Creek Wars, 62. *See also* Jackson, Andrew; Muscogee people

De Bow's Review (magazine), 89
deeds, 84–86
de la Rionda, Bernie, 119
Deyle, Steven, 70
Difficult Conversations (seminar), 142
Doing Our Own Work (DOOW), 3–5, 7, 8, 14, 31–39, 55–56, 144
Du Bois, W. E. B., 107

Easter (enslaved person), 71
Edmonds, Henry, 106–7, 108
Ella (enslaved person), 71
Emmanuel AME Church, 47
enslaved people: cemetery of, 65, 89; family separations, trauma of, 63, 70, 71, 72, 82, 84, 85, 86; mortgaging of, 70, 80–81, 85–86; sexual violence, threat of, 81, 83, 86; resistance by, 82–84

Ensley (AL), 96
Eslinger, Donald (sheriff), 119

Ferguson (MO), 129
Flescher, Ann, 56
Frankenberg, Ruth, 155n8, 161n17
Fulton, Sybrina, 115, 116, 119, 120

genealogy, 57–60, 137
George D. Shortridge Family Papers, 88
George Floyd protests, 133–35
Georgiana (enslaved person), 71
ghosts, 66
ghost walk, 63
Glymph, Thavolia, 79
Goldsby, Jacqueline, 96
Greensboro (NC), 21
Griffin (GA), 63
Guy, John, 119

Hallie Farmer Lecture, 68
Hannah-Jones, Nikole, 73, 86
Harjo, Joy, 72
Hawkins, James F. (sheriff, Jefferson County, AL), 103
HerStories Fest, 149
Hill, Marc Lamont, 117
Hillman Hospital (Birmingham, AL), 104
Hollums, E. L. (deputy, Jefferson County, AL), 103
Holly Brook plantation, 80, 82
hooks, bell, 114
Houston, Charles Hamilton, 105–6, 111
Howard University Law School, 105
Hughes, Langston, 107

Ifill, Sherrilyn, 97, 98, 99
Independent Monitor (Tuscaloosa, AL) 78
Indian Removal Act of 1830, 69, 78
indigenous dispossession, 69, 77–78, 136
in-reach, 155nb

Jackson, Andrew, 69, 72, 77, 78; 1830 Indian Removal Act, 69, 78; military campaigns against Muscogee, 77; efforts to remove insurgent Muscogee, 78. *See also* Muscogee people

Jefferson, Hakeem, 134
Jefferson County (AL) jail, 103
Jefferson County (AL) Sheriff's Department, 102
Jim Crow racism, 62, 73, 101–12
Johnson, Golda W., 61–62, 64, 76–77, 80, 84
Jones-Rogers, Stephanie, 79–80, 82
Jordan, Emma Coleman, 114, 121
Julia (enslaved person), 71

Kaufman, Gersh, 35
Kilby Prison, 103, 106
King, Edmund, 62–63, 67, 68–72, 80–82, 84–80
King, Martin Luther, Jr., 23–24, 111, 127–28
King, Nancy Ragan, 63, 65
King, Peyton, 72
King, Shelby, 71
King, Tom; 72
King, William, 72
King, William Rufus, 78
King family cemetery, 63, 64–65
King House, 7–8, 61–65, 68, 73, 75, 76–77, 79, 80; as haunted house, 7–8, 66; narratives, forging new, 68, 76, 77
King Iron Works, 69, 76

Leaven (NGO), 1, 5, 31
Leaven Center (Lyons, MI), 5–6, 29
lesbian feminism, 149–50
Lillian E. Smith Center for the Arts, 113–14
Lincoln Memorial, 22
Lives and Times of Kingswood in Alabama 1817–1890, The, 61–62, 69, 76–77, 80, 84
Long, James M. (assistant solicitor, Jefferson County, AL), 103–5
Lorde, Audre, 17, 38, 113
Lucy (enslaved person), 71
lynching, 95–99, 101–12, 123; antilynching legislation, 114; Association of Southern Women for the Prevention of Lynching (ASWPL), 114; impact on white children, 98; intergenerational legacies of, 99; judicial lynching, 101–12, 123–25; of George Armwood, 97; of Matthew Williams, 97; role of white women in, 113, 114, 120–21; soul splitting in white spectators, 98

172   Index

Mantei, Rick, 119–20
March on Washington, 19–24
Margaret (enslaved person), 85–86
Martin, Tracy, 115, 116, 119
Martin Trayvon, 115–21
mass deportations, 136
mass incarceration, 120, 128
Matthews, Rev. (Jefferson County, AL), 104
McDuff, Fred, 103
McIntosh, Peggy, 15, 53, 54, 137
McKinney, Charles, 134
McNair, Everett, 19–22
McPherson, Charles A. G., 111
Menawa, 72
Michigan State University, 1, 41
Miles, Tiya, 72
Miller, Benjamin M. (governor, AL), 106, 111
Minerva (enslaved person), 71, 82
Montevallo (AL), 7–8, 61–64, 67–68, 76, 87, 89
Montevallo Community Remembrance Project, 73
Montevallo Legacy Project, 8
Morales, Aurora Levins, 57, 59, 67, 87, 137
Morrison, Eleanor S., 1–2, 4, 19–24, 31–32, 90
Morrison, George, 59
Morrison, Marie Shortridge, 62, 68, 80
Morrison, Toni, 66, 95
Morrison, Truman Aldrich, Jr., 60, 90, 106–7
Morrison, Truman Aldrich, Sr., 59–60, 95–99
Mountain Brook (AL), 62, 106, 107
Murder on Shades Mountain (Morrison), 63–64, 101–12
Muscogee people: auctions of ceded land, 78; Battle of Horseshoe Bend, 77; ceding land to the US government, 69; slavery expanded in dispossessed land, 77, 78; trails of tears, 78. *See also* Jackson, Andrew
Mussey, Bessie Morrison, 62, 64

NAACP, 105–6, 107, 111
National Civil Rights Museum, 95–96
Nelson, Debra, Judge, 115–16
New Morning Star Baptist Church (Birmingham, AL), 109, 110, 111

O'Donnell, P. (judge, Cleveland, OH), 123–25
Old Screamer Mountain (Clayton, GA), 114

O'Mara, Mark, 115, 116
oppression, 6, 14, 25–26, 58–59
organizational change, 33, 36

Peterson, Henrietta, 105, 109, 110
Peterson, Willie, 102–5
Poole, Harriet Morrison, 7, 61–62, 69, 96
Princess Anne (MD), 97–98

racism: dismantling systemic racism, 35, 45, 135, 140, 151; four levels of, 33, 43; institutional, 33, 36, 115; interpersonal, 36, 37–38; personal, 135–36; structural power 15, 25, 111, 129, 136, 151; systemic, 8, 33, 34, 128
radical genealogy, 57–60, 137
Randolph, A. Phillip, 24
reparations, 90
restorative remembering, 72–73
Rich, Adrienne, 149
Richardson, Nancy, 2, 138
Roof, Dylann, 47–48
Rose, Lillian Roybal, 17, 51, 138
Russell, Timothy, 124–25
Rustin, Bayard, 24

Sales, Ruby, 114, 143
Salisbury (MD), 97–98
Sanford County (GA), 117
Saunt, Claudio, 69
Savage, Monique, 42
"Scottsboro Boys," 102
Secessionist Convention of 1860, 66
Sely (enslaved person), 82
Shadow Lawn Cemetery, 110
Shelby County (AL), 68, 69, 77
Shelby County Circuit Court, 84–85
Shelby County Courthouse, 81
Shelby County Museum and Archives, 76, 81, 84
Shortridge, Elizabeth King, 66–68, 71, 80–82, 84, 87–91; as first white child born in Montevallo (AL), 66–68, 87; owner of six enslaved people, 82
Shortridge, George D., 66, 80–81, 84–86, 87–88; circuit court judge, 66; delegate to Secessionist Convention, 66; gubernatorial candidate, 66; mortgaging enslaved people, 80

slavery: as credit system, 70; as "geography of containment," 83; legacies, of, 8, 73, 86; manumission, 85; remembering and reckoning with, 73, 86
Smith, Clint, 76
Smith, Lillian E., 113–14
soul splitting, 81, 95–99, 136
Stallworth, Lynnette, 13–15, 17, 27–29, 141–42
Stand Your Ground laws, 115
Strait, Buck, 102
Sukey (enslaved person), 84–86, 89

Talladega College, 19
Taylor, Keeanga-Yamahtta, 134–35
Terry, Robert, 14
Thomas, Clarence, 115
Thomas, Norman, 23
To Kill a Mockingbird (Lee), 108, 112
Trump, Donald, 134
Tuscaloosa Manufacturing Company, 78–79

United States Supreme Court, 105–6
Universities Studying Slavery (consortium), 73
University of Alabama at Birmingham (UAB), 109
University of Montevallo, 7–8, 63–64, 73, 89; Hallie Farmer Lecture, 68; Peace and Justice Studies Program, 1, 8, 75; "Why We Must Remember" conference, 61, 86, 89
University of Virginia, 73

Vietnam War, 127–28

Walker, Alice, 143
Weatherford, William, 63. *See also* Chief Red Eagle
Wells-Barnett, Ida B., 114

West, Don, 115
white ally work: accountable relationships, developing, 43–45, 141–43; ancestral legacies, investigating, 57–60, 137; collaborating with BIPOC, 16, 25, 26, 45; humility, 7, 8, 16, 26, 42, 142; cultural background identity, 51–56, 58–60; fear, move through 3, 9, 137–38; guilt, move through 9, 16–17, 26, 139; grief, acknowledge, 17, 26, 34, 35, 137–38; racial identity work, 14–15, 149–51; racism, confronting, 139–41; qualities and commitments, 25–26; self-love and joy, cultivating, 9, 17, 143–44, 146; shame, dealing with, 3, 9, 16–17, 26, 34–35, 137–39; social segregation, move out of, 9, 141; truth-telling relationships, nurture, 9, 16, 26, 141–43; white privilege, interrupting, 15–16, 136–37
white privilege, 15–17, 26–29, 45, 53, 55, 136–38
white supremacist backlash, 73, 134–35
white supremacy, 42, 45, 58, 87, 99, 105, 107, 111, 114, 128, 136, 147; intergenerational legacies of, 99, 138
white women: as enslavers, 70, 79–82
will and estate papers, 70–72
Williams, Augusta, 101–2, 109
Williams, Clark, 104
Williams, Dent, 103–4
Williams, Malissa, 124–25
Williams, Nell, 101–4, 109
Williams, Robert, 70
Wilson, Darren, Officer, 129
Wilson, Jesse, 78
Wilson's Hill, 78
Women's Theological Center (WTC) Anti-Racism Training Program, 1, 2–3
Wood, Jennie, 101, 109
Woolf, Virginia, 150

Zimmerman, George, 115–18, 120

www.ingramcontent.com/pod-product-compliance
Lightning Source LLC
Chambersburg PA
CBHW031320160426
43196CB00007B/595